GW01246594

THE
'PARENTING TEENAGERS'
PROGRAMME

Leader's Guide

by Michael and Terri Quinn

FAMILY CARING TRUST

First published 1988
by Family Caring Trust
8 Ashtree Enterprise Park
Newry
Co. Down
BT34 1BY

Illustrations by John Byrne
Copyright © Family Caring Trust 1988
Reprinted 1990

Revised edition © Family Caring Trust 1998
Printed by Universities Press (Belfast)
ISBN 1 872253 15 6
Reprinted with minor changes 2001

All rights reserved. No part of this publication
may be reduced, stored in a retrieval system
or transmitted in any form by any means, electronic,
mechanical, photocopying, recording or otherwise,
without the prior permission of the publishers.

CONTENTS

ABOUT THIS PROGRAMME
AND HOW IT WORKS

Materials

The materials for running the course are:

1. This *Leader's Guide*.
2. A video cassette
3. A *Handbook* for participants.

The Leader's Guide contains all the information needed for setting up the programme and conducting each session of it. (Individual items can always be supplied separately, but two copies of the *Guide* are supplied in the boxed kit because we encourage *two* facilitators to run the sessions.

The Video provides a short input (usually about 15 minutes) for each of the sessions.

The Parent's Handbook contains more detailed input and examples, table summaries of each chapter, and the various exercises for getting in touch with the topics, discussion, skill practice and planning. Each participant needs a copy of the *Handbook*. They are asked to read a short section of it between sessions. The reading matter is useful for reinforcing the learning both between sessions and long after a course has finished.

How the programme works

This is the *Leader's Guide* for running a six-week community programme for parents, followed by (if possible) a session for their teenagers and then a final 'follow-up' session for the parents a few weeks later.

Each session lasts for up to two hours and generally follows the order below (times are approximate, and you need have no qualms about shortening or leaving out an exercise, for it may be difficult at times to get through everything in two hours).

1. Introduction/Warm-up (up to 5 mins)

This is an opportunity to make everyone welcome, particularly anyone who, for whatever reason, may feel on the fringe of the group.

After the welcome, the leader explains simply and briefly what is going to happen during the session. When dealing with adults, it is best to involve them in what is happening as much as possible and not to have surprises.

Some kind of ice-breaking exercise can also be helpful, so there are some suggestions for warm-up activities for each session.

2. How everyone got on since the previous meeting (15-30 mins)

This is a chance for them to speak of their experiences during the previous week, particularly how they got on at home with what they had planned from the previous session. It is not essential to stick to the topic - parents often have other significant things to report, and it is enough that they are speaking personally. This kind of personal 'sharing' is probably the most valuable part of the entire course: it is disarming to hear a parent talk of 'failures' with children, and that encourages others to trust the group as well. On the other hand, hearing of another parent's improvements is usually more convincing than anything the leader might say and is both inspiring and empowering for parents.

The leader's role during this part of the session is to create an atmosphere of trust, to encourage efforts and improvements - and to use a little active listening to give members of the group a sense of being understood.

3. Getting in Touch (5-10 mins)

The topic is introduced with a short involving exercise (the 'Getting in Touch' section towards the end of each chapter of the handbook). That helps to get parents in touch with the topic of the session and to apply it to themselves. When they have had a minute or two to do the 'Getting in Touch' exercise, they can talk about it together for a further minute or so. This discussion is probably best done in small groups of two or three, so that more people get a chance to hear their own voices early in the session.

4. Introducing the topic (15-20 mins).

The topic is introduced, based on the video and on the table at the end of the relevant chapter of the *Handbook*. It is not recommended that you run the course without the video. Parents are also encouraged to read the short chapter from the handbook in advance. Because of poor reading

skills, time-pressures, etc., some parents will not have done this reading -
and that is okay - but the reading, when done, reinforces their learning.

After watching the video, parents may like to read briefly through the
table at the end of the chapter for a minute or so. They can then be
encouraged to comment, ask questions, react to the new ideas, and apply
the ideas to their own families. If they disagree with something, the
leader should not argue with them but might summarise or reflect back
what they say in a genuine effort to understand (though not necessarily
agree with) their point of view. The leader does not need to defend any of
the ideas and should be happy to see people thinking for themselves: that
makes for a healthy group.

5. Case Studies (up to 10 mins).
The Case Studies (previously presented on audiotapes) apply the new
input to typical family situations and are discussed to help deepen
people's understanding of the topic. They are probably the least important
part of a session and might be omitted now that there is a video to drive
home the input more clearly. If you do use them, consider cutting them
short, otherwise there may not be enough time for the skill practice,
planning and subsequent exercises – which tend to provide more
significant learning.

6. Improving your skills (usually 20-30 mins, sometimes longer)
Parents then have an opportunity to practise and improve their skills.
Some people find this the most helpful part of the meeting. That needs to
be said, because leaders sometimes skip this section, not appreciating its
value.

The skill practice needs to be well planned. During some sessions there
is a little role-play, for example, and while some people have a natural
gift for this, others have difficulty entering into it. This needs to be borne
in mind on the one or two occasions when volunteers are chosen in
advance for this kind of exercise. No one should be put into situations
that they are not reasonably comfortable with. After role play, a little
time also needs to be allowed to de-role - participants become aware of
the room they are in, relax and come out of any argument or role they
were in, and they remind themselves that they are not in that role
anymore.

7. **Planning to apply the ideas in the week ahead** (5-10 mins)

This is an opportunity for everyone to plan how they might apply the ideas from the meeting at home (there are some suggestions at the end of each chapter). They might take a minute or two in silence to write or tick what they plan to do - or they can plan together in couples or pairs. You can point out that they will have an opportunity at the beginning of the following week's session to tell the group how they get on with their plans. That can also be an incentive to putting the ideas of the course into action.

8. **Relaxation and Reflection** (about 5 mins)

Lights are dimmed and music is played while the parents learn methods of relaxation which may prove useful at home. They are also led through a short reflection which tends to reinforce the ideas from the session.

For churches and other interested groups, there is also an *option* of a brief religious dimension for use at this stage. This is for the two major religious groupings in Britain and Ireland - there is a Christian option and an Islamic one. You will find the Christian option in Appendix 1 at the back of this book, and the Islamic dimension is supplied free of charge on request. If you wish to include a religious element, it is respectful to prepare people by telling them about it in advance. When they are not taken by surprise, they are usually open to participating more fully.

You have permission to tape these Reflections if you wish - this could facilitate their use in the reflective atmosphere of a darkened room.

9. **Summing up and feedback** (5-10 mins)

A brief summing up of the session is followed by some feedback from the group on their experience of the session. This can be valuable in offering parents a chance to say how they are feeling, clarify what they have gained from the session and learn from what others have gained. The feedback is generally positive, but it can also offer a chance to express negative feelings like disappointment, confusion, etc. And it gives useful feedback to the leader. If there is little time, you can ask members of the group to be brief, even to name their strongest feeling at that moment.

10. **Concluding remarks** (1-2 mins)

The leader concludes the meeting by asking for a volunteer to bring the snack for the following meeting and by encouraging the parents to practise the skills and read the new chapter during the coming week. The reading is not essential but is worth encouraging because it can provide a useful reinforcement of the learning.

Sessions usually end with socialising over a cup of tea or coffee. It helps to *start* the first session with a cup of tea or coffee - that can be part of the welcome and it allows for latecomers. For subsequent meetings, it may be better to start punctually and have a simple snack *after* the session. That allows parents with commitments to skip the snack and get home quickly if they wish to do so. And, more importantly, it gives the parents an opportunity to chat and talk out things that have arisen during the meeting. It is suggested that responsibility for the snack be rotated among the participants - which ties in with the emphasis in the programme on self-help.

Evaluating what is happening

The structure of this programme, particularly the 'sharing' sections of each session, provides facilitators with continual qualitative evaluation, including specific examples of changes in family relationships. The usefulness of this should not be underestimated.

Researchers have discovered, however (including Patterson, Reid and Dishion, 1992), that what parents *report* about their interactions with their children does not always correspond with their *observed* behaviour. (This is another good reason for *including* teenagers in this programme.) So the Trust now plans to commission an extensive evaluation of the newly-revised programme, attempting to measure specific changes in attitude and behaviour, including changes in participants' ability to use the skills taught during the course - de-escalation, listening with openness, speaking more positively, conflict management, etc.

We also encourage you to take time with your co-facilitator after each session to reflect on your own facilitating and what is happening in the group. This is provided for in the *Facilitator's Guide* and need not be very academic, but it will let you know how well you are meeting people's needs. Part of it is just being aware of what happens during each session as you listen to and watch people's reactions to the various sections, as you gather feedback from them, and as you listen to comments they make. You are encouraged to adapt the course in the light of this feedback.

HOW THIS PROGRAMME WORKS

Theoretical Base

This course is not better than other parenting courses, but it may be different in that the emphasis is not on psychology or information but on teaching *skills* and making changes to the power base within the family. The emphasis on skills may go some way to explain its popularity with people from different social backgrounds (over seventy thousand people have taken the course in just over a decade).

Parenting programmes as we know them today began to develop in the US in the 1970s. They tended to grow out of and be closely linked with specific schools of psychology and their associated value systems. Family Caring Trust was able to benefit from studying the strengths and weaknesses of these US initiatives and to draw on their experience and research bases. These ideas were incorporated into a flexible programme which uses established principles of adult learning while emphasising 'good enough parenting' so as not to create inappropriate guilt.

No one parenting model is espoused by the Trust. Parents, for example, might adopt quite a directive and supervisory role when introducing young people to new skills or tasks, whereas they might adopt a more democratic and less directive role as their children grow in confidence and skill. This course is eclectic, then, not rigidly tied to any one system but drawing on **Adlerian psychology** (goals of misbehaviour, discipline through natural and logical consequences), **Bowen Family Systems** (emphasis on changing self rather than others, growing in self-differentiation and becoming a more non-anxious presence, also on reinforcing change by withdrawing attention from the more symptomatic elements in the family system and focusing on the more influential elements), **Reality Therapy** (negotiating and conflict management within the family), and **Person-centred Counselling** (active listening, expressing needs and feelings in "I" messages).

The Trust has also drawn on the work of established researchers and writers. Among them we would like to acknowledge:

Dr Don Dinkmeyer and Dr Gary McKay, whose STEP-Teen Programme has introduced Adlerian concepts in a practical and attractive format to a great many American parents.

Dr Edwin Friedman, whose explanation of Bowen Family Systems Theory helped us to see the importance of parents working at becoming more genuine *persons* with clearer boundaries and a clearer sense of who they are. Family Systems also provided a helpful overall context for healthy family functioning with its joint emphasis on Connectedness (keeping in touch and connected with young people) and Respect for Difference (allowing young people to <u>be</u> different, to have their own identity).

Dr Thomas Gordon, whose Parent Effectiveness Training programme has introduced parents to Active Listening and 'I' messages for more than a generation.

Dr John Gottman, for many insights, particularly his highlighting of the importance of de-escalating, non-defensive listening and speaking, and generally creating safety for a teenager to surface submerged needs and have them respected. (For many years we have acknowledged our debt to Haim Ginnott whom Dr Gottman also acknowledges as a major influence.)

Dr Howard Markman - the research he and his colleagues have conducted from the Dept. of Marital and Family Studies at the University of Denver has helped to convince us of the appropriateness of concentrating on skills for conflict management not only to deal with tensions but as an effective way to build family relationships.

Other important influences include Dolores Curran, Rudolf Dreikurs, Gerard Egan, Eric Ericson, Mary Pipher, Virginia Satir, Ron Taffel, Donald Winnicott and Patty Wipfler.

We also want to express our debt to all the people and organisations who contributed to the development and shape of this course or advised us on content, methodology and style. We are particularly grateful to Brendan McAllister, Director of the Mediation Network of Northern Ireland, and his co-workers, Naomi and John Lederach; who introduced us to some of the excellent work in conflict management being done internationally under the influence of the Graduate School of Conflict Analysis and Transformation at the Eastern Mennonite University of Virginia. Also to Dr John Coleman and Dr Debi Roker of the Trust for Study of Adolescence; the review of the literature on parenting adolescents which they undertook on our behalf helped to give us some new leads and a clearer sense of direction.

HOW TO BEGIN

It can be a little scary to look at the Leader's guide of a community programme if you have not already experienced the programme for yourself. This is not a complicated programme, however, and the purpose of this book is to lead you through it step by step.

Finding the participants

A group usually consists of eight to twelve parents. It may be best not to exceed this number, for participants learn a great deal from each other as trust builds up in the intimacy of a small group.

In general, parents doing the course should have at least one child thirteen years or older - or even a twelve-year-old who is displaying what is seen as teenage behaviour. They will usually get more from the programme, however, if they have already taken our general 'Fives to Fifteens' parenting course. Couples also tend to get more out of the course if they attend together, so that might be encouraged. It is particularly helpful to recruit parents of young people in the same *year* at secondary school because of the bond that creates between them and because it will be more attractive for the young people to attend the session for teenagers if they are about the same age.

It has been encouraging to see how well parents from different social backgrounds mix and bond together. Community development workers also suggest that we include lone parents or parents whose children have disabilities or special needs - rather than create special interest groups.

If people feel under *pressure* to attend a course, they will tend to get much less out of it. They need to come freely and willingly - in response to an information evening, an advertisement or an invitation from a friend, church or other agency - or from their teenager's school (a sample letter from a school principal has been included at the end of this book and might be adapted as you think fit).

Where courses are run

When possible, meetings should be held in comfortable, pleasant surroundings - a home might be quite suitable if it is reasonably free from distractions. Many leaders of groups have commented on the breaking down of social and other barriers and the growth in community spirit that occurs during a course - and experience shows that people learn better when this sense of community is present. A closer bond is often built and a greater community spirit created when a group meets in someone's home rather than in a school or institutional setting. Not every home is suitable, but that experience is worth considering.

Courses have also been run in community centres, parish halls, school libraries, staff-rooms, even classrooms. For obvious reasons, a classroom is not ideal - but we do not always have an ideal setting.

Keeping attendance up

It is reasonable to expect a fall-off of one to two people after the first session, although it often happens that there is no fall-off. Sometimes a parent misses a meeting and thinks that too much ground has been lost. Other parents may need a little encouragement. If parents miss a meeting, then, it may be a good idea to phone them to say how much they were missed and to enquire about them. But it is not a good idea to spend time chasing after people who are missing consistently or who are just not interested in continuing.

How often to meet

There are so many relatively new skills taught on the course that parents sometimes react to meeting weekly. A week does not seem to give them enough time to integrate the ideas and practice the skills. The truth is that it can take many years to become at ease with these skills, so there is something in these parents' objections. When we experimented with meeting at longer intervals, however, less seemed to happen between sessions. The impetus of regular meetings seems to be a valuable part of the learning process.

Finding and training leaders

Leaders of this course do not need specialised knowledge of parenting or child development. They are not expected to be 'experts' or to give input, for the input is in the video, the handbook and this Guide. Most leaders are ordinary parents, though they do not even have to be parents: many excellent courses have been run by single people. What seems to be more important is that they be good listeners and have a genuine respect for parents' experience, for their differences, and for their natural instinctive wisdom. Leaders are also expected to have a belief in the principles of the programme and a willingness to keep applying the new skills both in the group and in their own relationships.

There tend to be one or two potential leaders in every group - they will often stand out because of their commitment to practising the skills between sessions and their respect for differences. At the end of a course, you might ask someone like that to assist you in running your next course. They will then need to become familiar with the programme materials, especially this Guide. After a few sessions of the subsequent course, you can begin to fade into the background as the assistant leader feels confident enough to take over the running of the session. There is probably no better way to acquire the skills taught on this programme than to be supported in actually leading a group. And it is particularly encouraging to see how many statutory and voluntary organisations and churches have been providing practical ongoing training for their facilitators, thereby answering an important need today.

A nationally recognised, accredited training
For any organisation interested in providing a nationally recognised accredited training for group facilitators, there is a pack for training facilitators in the use of Family Caring Trust's parenting programmes. It has been developed by Susan Tym and Denis Drury of Hallam Caring Service, Sheffield, in co-operation with people from the Education, Health, Social Service and Voluntary sectors. The pack offers a ready-made tool for training group facilitators, with accreditation by the **Open College Network** at Level 3. Organisations in the UK and Ireland can use this resource to provide an accredited training for people wishing to facilitate the Trust's parenting programmes (and also to accredit the learning of the parents at levels 1 or 2, if they wish). For further detail you may like to visit our website at www.familycaring.co.uk (look under Training on the menu).

THE LEADER'S ROLE

We have just had a short summary of how the programme works. That gives some indication of what is expected of you as a leader. Let's take a look at that in more detail now.

One of the most important things a leader can do is to create a friendly and caring atmosphere. Your welcome, the cup of tea or coffee, your ongoing concern for and interest in the parents can do a great deal to relax them and to build a sense of community and caring in the group. And the more relaxed people are the better they tend to learn.

Not as an expert

During this course it does not help to act as an expert or teacher or to encourage parents to look to you for answers. They may find some answers in the video, in the parent's handbook, in the recommended reading and in what other members of the group have to say. Basically, however, parents need to see that each one is different, that other people's answers may not work for them, that they have to find their own answers. So you might answer their questions with:

"What do you think yourself?" "What does the book say about that?" or "Has anyone else any experience of this?"

Even if members of the group disagree on an issue, the leader is best not to come up with a 'solution' but to help them to move on. You might say something like: "I can see you both feel strongly about this, and it's an interesting point. It certainly shows how different things work for different people. I wonder though if we shouldn't move on and we might talk more about this over the cuppa after the meeting?"

Using the same skills as the parents

One of the most helpful things the facilitator can do is encourage. You might remind a discouraged member of the group, for example, "Well, you must feel discouraged about that, but how does the way you handle it now compare with the way you used to handle it?" Part of your task is to keep listening for efforts, strengths and improvements, and to reflect them back to the parents in a sincere, honest way.

THE LEADER'S ROLE

That brings us to a vital leadership skill - listening. Your success in leading the group will depend much more on how you listen than on how you talk. One of your tasks is to give people a sense of being understood, even if they are attacking basic elements of the course. If someone thinks that 'active listening' is merely opting out of effective discipline of teenagers, for example, it will not help to argue; it *will* help if you can grasp what they are saying and check if you have understood that correctly. In that way you are neither agreeing nor disagreeing and you are respecting the person who is objecting. Participants who have a sense of being listened to can feel free to change and grow at their own pace.

Another great quality you can bring to the group is your honesty about your own family. You can help to build up the vital trust level in the group by sometimes speaking first during the 'How we got on' section at the beginning of a session. When you let people hear about some of the difficulties and failures in your own family relationships (with due discretion), that can allow them to open up and risk talking about their own difficulties. When a group seems to be getting bogged down in discussion, too, it can help to talk about yourself and your family in relation to the topic being discussed. That helps to draw people away from theory and back to their own family situation. This should not be used as a licence for over-talking. Your main role is to lead by listening and encouraging.

You may notice that the skills a facilitator requires are exactly the same skills as the *parents* learn on this course - encouragement, listening, I-messages, etc. Anyone in a leadership position will tend to find these skills useful in everyday life - parents, teachers, managers, clergy, group facilitators...

Dealing with over-talkative people

If a parent begins to hog a meeting, you might say something like, "Well, I'm anxious to get through the programme for the evening, so I think we'll have to move on now, but what Margaret is talking about is an interesting point, so maybe we can come back to it over the cup of tea afterwards..."

Better still, you might use the group itself to restore order and to keep to the schedule if you cut in on someone with, "I'm sorry to interrupt you, Joe, but I suppose I'd like to ask the group if they want to deal now with this point - or would they prefer to move on to the next part of our programme for the evening?" You might also keep involving different people with: "Would you like to comment on that, Tom?" or "What do you think of that, Phil?" or "Why do you think that is so difficult for parents, Betty?" It is important, however, not to hop onto someone who is shy or who finds it difficult to talk in the group.

One way to draw timid people into the group and at the same time to control over-talkative people is to take the over-talkative person aside before or after the meeting and ask for help in drawing the shy person out. Giving that responsibility can help both of them.

The need for flexibility

Throughout this Leader's Guide there is a suggested script, giving the actual words which the leader can use to introduce a section or to link sections together. This may be useful for people who are inexperienced in facilitating groups, but it should only be used in so far as it is *helpful*. Please feel perfectly free to ignore it. You may be able to explain things more simply in your own words.

Finally, it is important not to be rigid but to be present to the members of the group and allow them all to use or adapt whatever ideas seem to suit *them*. When you are flexible and adaptable - open to different approaches and different experiences - a group tends to make better progress and individual parents tend to feel better about themselves. It can help to remember that there are no rules for parenting. Just guidelines. And guidelines don't apply always or in the same way to everyone.

Be flexible, too, in the use of group work - it depends so much on the number of people in your group, on their background and experience. Shy people may be frightened of speaking in a group of ten people but happy to chat away in twos or threes (when you are trying to keep an eye on the clock, you may also find it easier to interrupt two or three small groups than to cut in on a single group). At the same time something is missing when people are not exposed to the wider group. See if you can strike a balance, using your own judgement rather than rigidly following the suggestions in this Leader's Guide. This applies particularly after running the course once or twice. As you grow in confidence and experience, you may discover better ways of helping parents to learn. We are always pleased to hear from group leaders about their experiences, both their difficulties and their breakthroughs, and we would like to incorporate into future editions any ideas that seem to work for you.

SESSION ONE

CHECKLIST: Materials
Leader's Guide.
Handbooks (one per person,
including facilitators)
Newsprint - see section 1 below
Pencils or pens (preferably pencils)
Video player and cassette - pre-set.
Simple snack: biscuits and tea/coffee.
Music/ reading lamp for reflection

**CHECKLIST: To be done before
session begins**
Set videocassette at correct position
and volume.
Guide and Handbook open or marked
at relevant sections.
Music and reading lamp plugged in
and ready for operation.

Before the first meeting
Before the first meeting it helps to arrange the chairs in an informal,
circular fashion with no classroom overtones. Go through the checklist to
make sure you have everything you need for the session. Pencils are
preferable to pens, because parents can decide later, if they wish, to rub
out any ticks or notes they have made. A rough poster can be made out in
advance - with the questions for introductions (see section one) - or these
questions can be written on slips of paper, one for each threesome.

The first meeting follows a slightly different format to the other sessions
as people will first need to be introduced to each other and to the general
format of the programme.

1. Introduction (10-12 mins)
Make everyone welcome and explain the aim of the course. Something
like:

**I'd like to start by thanking you for coming this evening, for caring
enough about your young people to want to improve as parents and
for your generosity in giving up your time to do that. Anyone who
feels a bit shy is especially welcome because you've had the courage to
come along in spite of your feelings. I think you'll find it relaxing and**

I assure you that you won't be put into any kind of uncomfortable situation.

This is called the "Parenting Teenagers" Programme - but it also applies to any young people beyond their teens who may still be living in your home. It's a programme for ordinary parents - if people have very serious problems, like a son or daughter who's on hard drugs or who's an alcoholic, they may need to go to an agency or to people with special expertise in dealing with drugs or drink or whatever. But if we're an average group of parents of teenagers, I'm sure it's true to say that we all have problems of one kind or another - we wouldn't be normal otherwise.

The purpose of this course is to improve the way we get along with our teenagers, to learn to communicate better with them, to discipline them and so on. I think you'll find it practical - it certainly won't be just theory - and there'll be plenty of opportunities to apply the ideas and to practice the skills. The aim is to become more effective as parents in dealing with our teenagers and to encourage a growing sense of responsibility and co-operation in them.

I'd like to make it clear from the beginning that I'm not here as an expert on parenting. My job is to operate the video and to move through the different sections of the evening and help parents to come up with their *own* solutions. Every parent is different, your family backgrounds are different, your teenagers are all different - and nobody knows them as well as you do. There is not just one recipe for bringing up children. The input for the course comes from the video and from the book, not from me, and you can apply it in any way you like. I want you to feel perfectly free to ignore anything that wouldn't suit your family.

We'll start then by getting to know each other. I know that some people hate going round the circle and saying their names and so on, so it might be more enjoyable and relaxed if we can just form into small groups of three or four people. I'd like you all to get to know each other, so it's probably best to choose people whom you don't know, or at least people whom you don't know well. Here are some questions that you might like to chat about in order to begin to get to know each other - your name, where you're from originally, the number of children you have and what stages they're at. Then

perhaps you might like to talk about what you would like to gain from this course, and, if you have any fears, you could mention them too. I would ask you to make sure that everyone gets an opportunity to speak about each of the questions - you could take them one at a time and go around your group. So we'll take five minutes now just to begin to get to know each other.

A piece of newsprint can be put up on the wall (or a slip of paper can be given to each threesome) with the questions for discussion. You may need to help form groups. This exercise usually changes the atmosphere by helping to break the ice and allow people to relax. The questions are:

What is your name?
Where do you come from originally?
How many children do you have, and what stages are they at?
What would you like to gain from this course?
What fears do you have about the course?

2. How meetings are run (5 mins)

Explain how the sessions work. Something like this:

Well, as your probably know, we'll have six weekly meetings, each lasting up to two hours. We start each meeting by talking about how we got on since the previous meeting - we usually have planned certain things to try with our teenagers and it's interesting to hear what happens when parents do try something different. You'll also be given some pages of this parent's book to read each week and you may want to disagree with something or make a comment on what you've read - that will get us into the new topic for that evening. Then we watch a section of the video for about fifteen minutes, and you may like to discuss in twos or threes how the input from the video might apply to a couple of typical family situations. Next, we take time to *practise* a parenting skill, and then we take a few minutes to plan what we can do to apply that skill in our families during the week ahead. Finally, we change the atmosphere by playing instrumental music and offering you a chance to take a few moments to calm down and be quiet and reflect. I'll give out the books now... Could you start by turning to the back of the book and looking at the *Agreements* or *Groundrules*. I'll

read them aloud so that we stay together, and you can make any comments you wish when we've finished reading them.

Distribute the books unless participants already have them. As with all the exercises in the *Handbook*, it is suggested that you read the guidelines aloud if you suspect that some participants may have poor reading skills - otherwise, allow a minute or two for everyone to read the Groundrules in silence. Then ask if the members of the group are happy with the Groundrules, or is there anything else they might like to add.

During the course, it may be necessary to come back to these Groundrules occasionally and highlight one that is being ignored.

3. Getting in Touch (5-10 mins)

The 'Getting in Touch' exercise that follows is useful for drawing parents into the course at a personal level - *talking at a personal level is much more helpful in enabling people to change than merely discussing ideas.* By the end of the exercise you will probably notice a marked increase in trust and safety in the group.

We'll begin this section by taking a few minutes to do the 'Getting in touch' exercise at the end of Chapter One. You're asked to put a tick beside anything in that list that you'd like to be more effective in dealing with. (Consider reading the list aloud.)

After a minute or two:

It can be hard to choose just *one* area to work on, but will you try underlining one or two things that you'd like to concentrate on...

After a further minute or so:

Now, maybe you'd like to chat together in twos or threes, especially about the things in that list that annoy or bother you most...

Consider reading the exercise aloud. Then, after two minutes:

And just to get an idea, I wonder if some of you would tell me one or two of the things you marked...

There can be great safety in a group when we hear others acknowledge that they too have some difficulties with their teenagers.

4. Introducing the topic (15-20 mins).

The video section for Session One may now be played. If you do not have the video, you might summarise the ideas in chapter one in your own words, basing what you say on Table 1, but it is not recommended that you run the course without the video as considerable impact is lost without it.

After watching the video, encourage the participants to chat in pairs for a minute or so about their reaction to it (the chatting is best done in pairs and not in the full group for the first few sessions, so that shy people don't feel threatened). After a minute or so:

Would anyone like to make a comment about the video, or say how these ideas might apply in your family...?

If people react, or are critical of the ideas, please respect their right to disagree, and do not argue or defend the ideas. You might say something like: *"Yes, some people don't find these ideas helpful - we're all different, and we're going to find that different things will help different people. So throughout this course, I want you to feel perfectly free to ignore whatever you don't find helpful."* Or you might say, *"Thanks for saying that. My job is not to defend any of the ideas on this course. The group is meant to help you make your own decisions, and I feel encouraged that you already feel free to state your own opinions. I can see it's going to be a healthy group."*

5. Case Studies (about 10 mins)

The Case Studies, previously presented on audio tapes, apply the new input to typical family situations and are discussed to help deepen people's understanding of the topic. They will be part of the Revised Parent's Handbook when it is published, but they are probably the least important part of a session and might be omitted now that there is a video to drive home the input more clearly. (If you choose to use the audio tapes, consider cutting them short or there may not be enough time for the skill practice - which tends to provide more *significant* learning)

6. Improving your skills (10-20 mins)

The next section of the evening can be introduced something like this:
Well, we've been looking this evening at ways in which we can avoid taking the bait, ways of breaking the unhelpful patterns of behaviour that we have been using perhaps all our lives. Let's try a little experiment now to illustrate that. Will you fold your arms in the way you usually fold your arms in front of your chest... Now notice how they're folded. We all have our own way of being comfortable. Some people tuck in their left hand, others their right hand, whatever.

Now, will you try folding your arms in the opposite way... (doing it yourself) **This is just as good a way to fold your arms, but it doesn't *feel* as comfortable... Maybe it helps to illustrate how we tend to act, without thinking, in little *patterns* of behaviour. That is not a bad thing - it means I don't have to make a new decision every time I want to do something. But *some* patterns are not helpful, maybe especially for parents. It may be a habit or an attitude we picked up from our own parents and we fall back on it when there's a problem - we use the same tone of voice or the exact same words that our parents used, a kind of knee-jerk reaction. Or some of us react against the way we were brought up by doing the *opposite* to what our parents did. Both are unthinking patterns, and psychologists tell us that the first step in changing them is to become *aware* of them. So here's an exercise now to help us become aware.**

The suggestion is that you form pairs and talk for a few minutes about how your own parents or carers parented *you* - and how that has influenced you. Just share what you feel comfortable sharing. Ask yourself: "What was their style of parenting, and can I see ways in which I am influenced by them - either *similar* to them or reacting *against* them in the ways I deal with my own teenagers today?" If one of you would like to talk first in each pair, I'll give you a signal after about two minutes and the other person can then tell how *they* were brought up and how that influenced *them*...

This is more an *awareness* building exercise than a *skill* building one, but it eases people into working in pairs for future sessions.

Occasionally, this exercise may touch into painful memories, so it is important to keep it *short* and not have people get into deep feelings about their parents. Ask people to change around after two minutes, even though they may have much more to say.

When this exercise has been done, you might add:

Most people find it fairly easy and enjoyable to talk of their memories like this, but it's possible that a few of you may have found it painful. If it is *very* painful to look back on how you were parented, that may be an indication that you need to find someone to talk with - a counsellor or a friend who can listen well. As you free yourself a little from that pain, *you'll* be a happier person and your parenting can only improve as you free yourself from rigid patterns of parenting.

Any comments on that exercise - did any of you notice ways in which you were influenced by your own parents or carers...?

7. Planning for next week (7-8 mins)

This is an opportunity for everyone to plan how they will apply the ideas from Session One over the next week. They may need a little quiet time to do this. The section can be introduced something like this:

We've just seen that the first stage in making a change is awareness. The second stage is to make a *specific and little* plan, preferably *written down* - so we'll take a few minutes at the end of each session to plan how we're going to apply the ideas in our own families over the next week. You may like to take a minute or two now to look at the "Planning" section at the end of chapter one and to make some plans. It may also help to *write* what you plan to do. That way, you can be more specific, and you can look it up at home and remind yourself of what you've planned...

After about two minutes:

Maybe you'd like to talk in pairs about your plans now and to tell each other what you intend to do, because telling someone what you've planned usually helps to make it happen!

It may help if couples work together at this stage - even if you're planning completely different things...

After a further two minutes you might say:

The third and last stage in making a change is pretty obvious - to keep practising. Every day. Your new approach may feel awkward and unnatural at the beginning, and you may feel discouraged when things don't improve immediately. But that's normal. It takes time to break old habits and learn new skills, but they quickly become second nature.

It's usually interesting, when people come back on the second evening, to hear how they've got on when they tried taking a new approach with their teenagers, ignoring squabbling, listening instead of scolding, encouraging instead of nagging, withdrawing from fights or whatever, so I look forward to hearing that. There's no guarantee that what you're going to do this week will work, but it's only by experimenting and trying a different approach that you'll learn what *is* more effective.

I wonder would a few of you perhaps give us an idea of what it is you plan to do..?

A few contributions from people at this stage can be quite inspiring for others - and can help others revise their plans and become more specific.

8. Relaxation and Reflection (about 5 mins)

The reflection offers parents a time of calm towards the end of a session. They have an opportunity to reflect and to learn methods of relaxation (which can be part of their new strategy for dealing effectively with their anger). It helps to change the atmosphere in the room by lighting a reading lamp, extinguishing other lights, playing instrumental music softly in the background and speaking gently and softly as you continue:

Towards the end of each session, we usually have a quietening down time and a short reflection. I'll put on some background music to help you relax, and you're asked to sit comfortably, perhaps keep your back straight - close your eyes if that helps, and breathe more deeply... (pause) **and slowly...**

Some people may be uncomfortable with the relative silence, so it may help to interrupt the silence after thirty seconds as you remind them:

Just relax, breathing deeply... and slowly...

After a further 30 seconds, lower the music and continue:

Relaxing like this is something you might consider doing to relieve stress when you find yourself tense or angry with a teenager, or in *any* difficult situation - just, if possible, to sit down for a few minutes, and relax by breathing in and out more deeply. Each week we'll try different ways of relaxing so you'll find something that suits you.

Now read the following slowly, pausing for a little while each time you come to continuous dots:

I'd like you to think back for a few moments now to your own teenage years... Can you picture yourself...? What were your clothes like...? Remember your hair style...? How did you spend your free time...? Remember the dancing and the music...? What were your favourite songs...? Remember your friends, how you got on with them - both girls and boys..

Remember times when you were no angel... times when you got into trouble... Then there were lonely times too... and unpleasant feelings... Can you thing of times when you felt inferior... guilty...

embarrassed... awkward... **There were anxieties, confusion, doubts about yourself... and there was the scoffing and sarcasm of others...**

I wonder if life isn't even harder for young people today than it was for us... Were there the same exam pressures in our day? What were the chances of getting a job then...? Was there the same exposure to violence and sex...? Did you have the same worries or concerns about the future as today's young people have...? (Pause.)

It's no harm to remember that these are all part of our young people's world today. It might not be so nice for any of us to be thirteen or fourteen, or eighteen or nineteen again. (pause) **Thinking about all this can help us to appreciate something of our young people's world, some of their pressures and fears and insecurities, some of their excitement and their concerns.**

If you are using the optional religious dimension, you can let the music continue to play. The text for it is in Appendix 1 (Christian). An Islamic dimension is available on request from Family Caring Trust. Whether you are using the religious dimension or not, you might end:

You can open your eyes now and come back to the room gently when you're ready, and become aware of your surroundings again...

Let the music fade out gradually - do not switch it off abruptly.

9. Summing up and feedback (5-10 mins)

It is helpful to take some time at the end of a session to sum up briefly what has happened and allow parents to make a comment, express a thought or feeling, disagree with something or appreciate what they have gained. It is also a useful way of checking out what *has* been gained and of clarifying a point that may have been misunderstood. This section might be introduced something like this:

In this session we looked at ways of giving teenagers good attention but not giving attention on demand or in a knee-jerk, unthinking way. We saw that a clearer *awareness* of what we are doing helps to break unhelpful patterns and enables us to make a new start and begin to change. We then made some plans to give less attention on demand and begin to connect better with our young people.

So I wonder if we could have some feedback now on how you found the session. Feel free to say which part of it you were uncomfortable with, and what you found helpful...? Whatever occurs to you...

We owe it to parents to end the meeting at the agreed time. If you are short of time, it may be enough to ask:

I wonder if you'd like to say in *one* **word how you're feeling now at the end of this session - confused, relaxed, upset, hopeful, whatever...**

The sharing sometimes reflects a little resistance from one or two participants to having been put into groups of two or three during the session - "Why can't we just discuss things as a group and hear what everyone thinks?" It may help to explain that it is to ensure that shy people have a chance to talk - and that, as people relax, you'll be quite happy to open out the discussion to the full group.

If the sharing is a bit negative (which would be unusual), it will help to end on a positive note by also asking the participants to say one thing they feel they learned or gained.

10. Concluding remarks (1-2 mins)

Emphasise the value of reading the new chapter in advance of the next meeting. Something like:

I want to draw your attention to the usefulness of reading your handbook. It's simply written. There's no jargon, and it's a great help in reinforcing any of the ideas we meet. Each week you're asked to read the short chapter in preparation for the next session - it's just about four of five pages, so it's no big deal, but it does help. For next week we're asked to have chapter two read. I would also encourage those of you who haven't read chapter one to read it first.

I'd also like this to become your group and not my group. One thing that helps that to happen is when a different person takes responsibility each time for the snack. Now when I say 'snack' I mean a packet of biscuits and a pint of milk. If you prepare an elaborate snack, that puts pressure on the others to do the same thing. So please keep it simple. Could we have a volunteer for next week?...

I hardly need to remind you that practice is the key to success - those who make the greatest strides during this course are the ones who keep practising every day between sessions. So I look forward to meeting you all again next week and to hearing how you get on with trying a new approach. And thank you for your generosity and trust in coming along this evening.

After the meeting

It helps to take a few minutes to chat to your co-leader about how the session went, what you learned from it, and what you might do differently in future. Pay special attention to whether you answered questions instead of turning them back and encouraging parents to find their own solutions. Giving advice is *not* part of your role.

SESSION TWO

CHECKLIST: Materials
Your Leader's Guide.
Your Handbook
Pencils or pens (preferably pencils)
Video player and cassette - pre-set.
Simple snack: biscuits and tea/coffee.
Music/reading lamp for reflection

CHECKLIST: To be done
Set videocassette at correct position
and volume.
Music and reading lamp plugged in
and ready for operation.
Guide and Handbook open or marked
at relevant sections.

1. Introduction and warm-up (about 5 mins)
Make members of the group welcome. It may be useful to ask the group
to look once again at the guidelines at the end of their book and to
highlight one or two if they were ignored during the previous meeting:

**I'd like to make you all welcome this (evening). In this session we'll
be looking at listening, which many people think is the most necessary
of all skills that the parent of a teenager can have.**

**We began to get to know each other last week, and I'd encourage
you to sit beside different people each week, so you may like to change
seats now if you find you're sitting beside the same person as last
week... (pause) Maybe you'd like to begin by reminding everyone
what your name is and the age-range of your children...**

When all have introduced themselves, you might add:

**It's hard to remember all those names, so here's a game that can
help - Joe here says "I'm Joe". Next Susan says "I'm Susan and
that's Joe." Then Beth says "I'm Beth and that's Susan and That's
Joe" And let's see how far we can get...**

Help anyone who gets stuck - remembering the names is not as
important as the laughter and 'ice-breaking' that this exercise creates.

2. How everyone got on since the previous meeting (15-30 mins)
It helps to begin this section by recalling last week's plans. Don't be
afraid of silence, because many people need a little time to gather their

thoughts together before speaking. Your role is to encourage any efforts or improvements - you may even use your own active listening skills occasionally to reflect what someone says. You could introduce this section by saying something like:

Last week, we looked at ways of giving teenagers good attention but not giving attention on demand or in a knee-jerk, unthinking way. We saw that a clearer *awareness* of what we are doing helps to break unhelpful patterns and enables us to change and make a new start. Towards the end of the session we made some plans to give less attention on demand and begin to connect better with our young people. So I wonder how you got on with that, or how have things been in your family over the past week...?

The sharing during this section may be the most important part of the session. So it usually helps to set a headline by sharing something that you yourself have done. If you do, remember to be brief - and not to be too 'perfect'. Mentioning a mistake you made or something that didn't work out well will often be as helpful as mentioning a 'success.'

3. Getting in Touch (5-10 mins)

Well, thank you for sharing that with the group. We'll move on now to this evening's topic which is listening. Last week we saw how useful it can be to take a new approach with our teenagers, maybe even to do the opposite to what we normally do, and this week I think we'll see that one of the best ways to do that is just to be quiet and listen.

So we'll start by taking a few minutes to get in touch with the topic. I'll read aloud the first half of the 'Getting in touch' section at the end of Chapter Two and we'll see what memories it sparks off...

Allow just a minute or two for a few people to talk, but then move on to the more important *positive* experience of being listened to - read aloud the second half of the 'Getting in touch' exercise and ask for comments on that for a further few minutes.

4. Introducing the topic (15-20 mins).

The video section for Session Two may now be played. If you do not have the video, you might summarise the ideas in chapter two in your own words, basing what you say on Table 2, but it is not recommended that you run the course without the video.)

After watching the video, encourage the participants to chat in pairs for a minute or so about their reaction to it (the chatting is best done in pairs and not in the full group for the first few sessions, so that shy people don't feel threatened). After a minute or so:

Would anyone like to make a comment about the video, or say how these ideas might apply in your family...?

If people are critical of active listening, it is best not to try to defend it. Instead, try using your own active listening skill by saying something like: *You seem to be saying that you're not too happy with this approach because it seems a bit artificial and unreal to you (or because it seems like giving in to your teenagers).*

After a little discussion, you could move on to the *Case Studies* - or move directly to the *Skill Practice* in section 6.

5. Case Studies (about 10 mins)

The Case Studies, previously presented on audiotapes, apply the new input to typical family situations and are discussed to help deepen people's understanding of the topic. They are probably the least important part of a session and might be omitted now that there is a video to drive home the input more clearly. If you do use them, consider cutting them short, otherwise there may not be enough time for the skill practice, planning and subsequent exercises – which tend to provide more *significant* learning.

6. Improving your skills (20-30 mins)

Form the group into threes for the skill-building exercise, explaining that one will be a listener, one will be a speaker and one will be an observer. Something like this:

We'll move on now to practising the art of listening. I'm going to ask you to form into groups of three. If you have come as a couple, it's usually better to split up for this exercise.

If there are two people left over, you can take part in one of the groups; if there is only one left over, yours can be a twosome.

For this exercise you're asked to keep your books open at the checklist that follows Table Two. You can see there some signs of helpful listening. Maybe we'll take half a minute to look down through that checklist to see what those signs are...

Allow half a minute for people to read down through the checklist, and then continue slowly:

Next, I'd like you all to get in touch with a problem, imaginary or real, to talk about in your group. Not something major like your marriage breaking up! but preferably something real - maybe a worry about one of your children, or about work... or your health... or someone else's health... in-laws... Or perhaps a conflict you've had at some stage - or that you still have - with a neighbour... or a teacher... or a brother or sister who has stopped talking to you... But not something too intimate or painful... So you might describe the problem or conflict and how it built up and how you felt at the different stages, and perhaps what you did about it, and how you felt then and so on. Can you think of something...? (pause) Got it...?

Now one of you is going to be the speaker, the second will be the listener and the third will be the observer. You'll all have turns, so it doesn't matter who does what first. We'll take two or three minutes for the first speaker to talk about their problem and I'll give you a signal when the time's up. The listener's job is to say as little as possible and to do anything on that page you're holding to give the speaker a good experience of being understood and listened to. So please don't be jumping in to say: "That happened to me too." And whatever you do, don't offer suggestions or advice - just listen. Finally the observers - their job is to tick off, on the page, any signs of good listening they notice - do you need pencils...?

Can you decide now who's going to speak first, and as soon as you're in touch with a problem you'd like to talk about, you can start. I'll give you a signal in two or three minutes to stop talking.

Allow a few minutes from when people start talking, and then interrupt.

I'm sorry to interrupt you now, but could the *speakers* just mention anything that helped them to talk or helped them to have a sense of being listened to or understood, and then the observers can say what *they* noticed.

After a minute or two, continue:

I'd like you to switch around now. The listener now becomes the speaker, the speaker becomes the observer, and the observer becomes the listener. So if you're ready to start talking about a new problem or conflict, off you go...

The same process is repeated until everyone has had a chance to practise each of the three roles, if possible. Then ask for some feedback:

Well, what was that like? Listeners first - what made it difficult to listen, or what did you feel like saying...? (take some feedback.)

What about the speakers - what helped you to talk or to feel understood...? (take feedback.)

Now, I'm not suggesting you do something as formal as that with your teenagers, but I wonder if you see possibilities in what you've just done - anyone...?

7. Planning for next week (7-10 mins)

That brings us straight into the planning for next week. You've just had a few minutes of undivided attention from another person listening to you and the suggestion is that we might also give a few minutes of completely undivided attention to one of our teenagers during next week. Planning may help, but it's only part of the answer - with teenagers, the best times often occur when *they're* ready, not just when you're ready. But thinking about it and planning can make you more available and *readier* to listen and respond. So you could look at the section of your book 'Plans for next week' and take a minute or so to read that and plan quietly on your own what you might do to give someone a good experience of being listened to during the week. Timing is obviously essential - maybe when they're worried about something. And being specific helps - not asking "How's school?" so much as "Who's on the team?" or "Who was at the meeting?" You may like to write in the space provided as you plan, because that will help you to remember what you've planned...

After a minute or so you can continue:

Maybe you'd like to talk in pairs about your plan now and to tell each other what you intend to do. Couples may prefer to plan together at this stage.

After a further two minutes you could move on to the relaxation time.

8. Relaxation and Reflection (about 5 mins)

Change the lighting as usual and play music softly in the background. Read the following passage slowly, stopping briefly at the continuous dots.

SESSION TWO

We're going to change the atmosphere a little now (dimming lights, and lighting a reading lamp or candle) **so you could just make yourselves comfortable and relax, close your eyes or whatever helps, and take half a minute now to become aware of your breathing as you breathe more deeply and slowly...** (Music) **As you breathe slowly, let the relaxation spread through your body... Feel your feet on the ground relax. Feel your ankles and legs relax... Your knees... Let your thighs relax fully.., and your bottom and lower back... Feel the relaxation spread through your stomach, which carries so much stress... Now sense the relaxation in the entire lower half of your body... Relax your back now... And your chest... Your arms... Your hands... Your fingers... And let all the tension drain out of your shoulders, which is another area that carries a lot of stress... Then your neck... your face... your jaw... your forehead... Your head... Your whole body now...**

When you pull out of an argument with your teenager and take a break for a while, it's great to have some way to relax. Last week we tried breathing, this week becoming aware of the different sensations in our bodies. You'll know best what seems to help you.

If you are using the optional religious dimension, you can let the music continue to play for that short period. The text for the religious dimension is in Appendix 1 (Christian). An Islamic dimension is available on request from Family Caring Trust. Whether you are using the religious dimension or not, you might end:

You can open your eyes now and come back to the room gently when you're ready, and become aware of your surroundings again...

Let the music fade out gradually - do not switch it off abruptly.

9. Summing up and feedback (5-10 mins)

It helps to take some time at the end of a session to sum up briefly what has happened and allow parents to make a comment, express a thought or feeling, appreciate what they have gained or disagree with something. It is also a useful way of checking out what has been gained and of clarifying a point that may have been misunderstood.

In this session we've looked at the importance of listening, and at some ways of making our listening more effective. And we've made some plans to listen and connect better with our young people.

So I wonder if we could have some feedback now on how you found the session. Feel free to say what you were uncomfortable with and what you found helpful. Whatever occurs to you...

We owe it to parents to end the meeting at the agreed time. If you are short of time, it may be enough to ask:

I wonder if you'd like to say in *one* word how you're feeling now at the end of this session - confused, relaxed, upset, hopeful, whatever...

10. Concluding remarks (1-2 mins)

Ask for a volunteer to bring the snack for the following week and emphasise the value of reading the new chapter before the next meeting.

For next week we're asked to have chapter three read. And can we have a volunteer to bring the milk and biscuits for next week...?

Thank you. And I look forward to meeting you all again next week and hearing how you get on with your listening. Incidentally, we can practise these skills with other people - with partners or friends or workmates - they're not just to make us better parents . So we should have plenty of opportunities to practise them during the week.

After the meeting

Again the questions for your own evaluation:

Did I talk too much? Did I answer questions or did I toss them back to the group? Are group members beginning to look to themselves for answers or do they see me as the expert? Did any problems arise? Do I need to refer to one of the 'guidelines' next week, or how can I deal with the problem? Who needs encouragement?

SESSION THREE

CHECKLIST: Materials
Your Leader's Guide.
Your Handbook
Pencils or pens (preferably pencils)
Video player and cassette - pre-set.
Simple snack: biscuits and tea/coffee.
Music/ reading lamp for reflection

CHECKLIST: To be done
Set videocassette at correct position
and volume.
Music and reading lamp ready.
Guide and Handbook open or marked
at relevant sections.
Plan with 2-4 parents (see section 6)

1. Introduction/Warm-up (3-5 mins)

Make everyone welcome, especially anyone who missed last week's
meeting. Consider doing a warming-up exercise:

**Let's try a warm-up exercise to start with. If we all stand in a circle
first, I'll give you directions... Now, would everyone put both hands
into the centre of the circle and with each hand find someone else's
hand to hold - not the hand of someone beside you... There should be
no free hands - everyone holding one other hand in *each* hand. Okay,
now without letting go of anyone's hand, will you untangle yourselves
to form a circle once again... It's okay if some of you are not facing
into the circle...**

Stop the exercise if they have not disentangled after two minutes.

2. How everyone got on since the previous meeting (15-30 mins)

It helps to begin this section with a brief recap of the previous session.
When the sharing begins, don't be afraid of silence, because many people
need a little time to gather their thoughts before speaking. Encourage any
efforts or improvements - perhaps by using your own active listening
skills occasionally to reflect your understanding of what someone says.
You could introduce this section by saying something like:

**Last week, we were looking at Listening and the suggestion was that
we would try to make use of any opportunity that might come our way
to practise active listening with *anyone* who had strong feelings, but
especially with our children. There was also the suggestion that we
might have one good listening session with one of our teenagers during**

the week, so I wonder how you got on with that or how have things been in your families?

As before, it may help to share something that you yourself have done, remembering to be brief - and not to be too perfect. You can also encourage others to speak with open questions: "Was it hard to get started - to try something different..? What made it difficult..? What helped..?"

3. Getting in Touch (5-10 mins)

We'll move on now to this week's topic, which is encouragement. If you look at the 'Getting in touch' section at the end of Chapter Three, you might take a minute or two on the first exercise. I'll read it aloud slowly, and you can feel free to mark it with a pencil as I speak...

After reading it slowly, allow a few moments. Then:

You could move on now to the second exercise - the things you like about your teens - and take another minute or so on that.

After a minute or two:

Well, that's just to get us thinking at a personal level about the topic, so we're ready to move on to the video.

4. Introducing the topic (15-20 mins).

The video section for Session 3 may now be played. (If you do not have the video, you might summarise the ideas in chapter three in your own words, basing what you say on Table 3, but it is not recommended that you run the course without the video.)

After watching the video, encourage the participants to chat in pairs for a minute or so about their reaction - or open out the discussion to the wider group:

Would anyone like to make a comment about the video, or say how these ideas might apply in your family...?

If people react, or are critical of the ideas, please respect their right to disagree, and do not argue or defend the ideas. After a little discussion, you could move on to the case studies - or move directly to the skill practice in section 6.

5. Case Studies (about 10 mins)

The Case Studies, previously presented on audio tapes, apply the new input to typical family situations and are discussed to help deepen people's understanding of the topic. They are probably the least important part of a session and might be omitted now that there is a video to drive home the input more clearly. If you do use them, consider cutting them short, otherwise there may not be enough time for the skill practice, planning and subsequent exercises – which tend to provide more *significant* learning.

6. Improving your skills (20-30 mins)

Ask for two volunteers to be a (father) and a teenage daughter. It is better still if you have arranged with two people in advance about the role-play that follows now. When the role-play goes well on this first occasion, it provides a model and makes it easier for others to role-play during future sessions. (You will notice that we do not *use* the word *role-play* in the script as it is usually not helpful to use that *word*.)

Ask the two volunteers to sit together now. One will pretend to be a teenage girl and the other will be her father or mother. The parent is attempting to teach the daughter to wire an electric plug (or to drive a car - or to iron a pair of trousers - you decide). The daughter is more interested in varnishing her nails and thinking up objections to having to learn this. The parent does all the wrong things, scolding her, criticising her, etc.

If parents are reluctant to do this exercise, you might act as the parent yourself, but don't skip this skill-practice lightly, for it can have a powerful effect - as well as being good fun.

We'll move on now to practising encouragement. I've asked two volunteers to act as (father) and daughter, and the (father) is going to attempt to teach his daughter how to... The first time, he's going to do all the wrong things - criticising, nagging, etc. And his daughter, as you will see, is not going to be co-operative. Okay...?

Allow a minute or so for this exercise and then ask:

How did everyone feel during that? Maybe we'll start with the daughter - how did you feel...? And the parent - how did you feel...? And the rest of you - what was your reaction as you watched...?

Now I'm going to ask you to do it again, but this time I want you to be an understanding, encouraging parent. Make sure to find a suitable time to teach and to take a positive approach, and we'll see how that goes...

Again, allow a minute or so for this, and then ask (father) and daughter:

How did you feel this time...?
Anyone else like to make any comments...?
If there is time, move on to the second situation, this time a mother attempting to teach her son to scramble an egg. Again this situation is approached the wrong way first, the boy is resentful and the mother nagging, impatient and cross. Then it is done positively. After both attempts, ask how people felt and give them an opportunity to comment.

7. Planning for next week (7-10 mins)

The skill practice can lead naturally into the planning. If the sharing at the beginning of the session has indicated that little is happening between sessions, it may help to *say* you are disappointed that so few people had examples of putting last week's plan into action. You might point out that what happens between sessions is the key to the success of the course.

That brings us to the planning for next week. We've just been looking at ways of encouraging teenagers and helping to involve them in new responsibilities. You could look now at the section *Plans for next week* at the end of chapter three. The suggestion is that we plan ways of encouraging our most discouraged child - and also that we introduce at least one of our teenagers to one new responsibility during the next week. You could take a minute or two to read the suggestions there and to plan for next week. As usual, it may be a good idea to write down what you plan so that you remember what you've planned when you go home.

After one or two minutes you can continue:
Maybe you'd like to talk in pairs about your plan now and to tell each other what you intend to do. Couples may prefer to plan together at this stage.

After a minute or so you can continue:
I wonder if a few of you would like to tell us what you plan to do...?

After a further two minutes you could move on to the relaxation time.

8. Relaxation and Reflection (about 5 mins)

Change the atmosphere by lighting a reading light or candle and playing music softly in the background. Read the following passage slowly, stopping for about 15 seconds at each 'pause.'

We're going to change the atmosphere a little now (dimming lights, and lighting a reading lamp or candle) **so you could just make yourselves comfortable and relax, close your eyes or whatever helps, and take half a minute now to become aware of your breathing as you breathe more deeply and slowly...** (Music)

There is a story about a man who was walking along a street when someone tripped him with a stick. He felt a sudden flush of anger - until he looked up and saw that it was a white stick and the person who accidentally tripped him could not see. Immediately his feelings of anger changed and he became understanding. That can happen for all of us - when our attitude changes, our feelings change. It may be as simple as changing the way we look at a conflict we have with a teenager. If I think it's terrible that my daughter or son is being rebellious, I'm naturally going to be stressed. But if my attitude is "I don't like this, but it's normal for teenagers to rebel, and it's not the end of the world," then the stress is going to be much less... You can probably remember a time when your own feelings changed as soon as you began to look at a situation differently... (pause)

Over the past few weeks, we've been looking at ways that help us cope with the almost inevitable stresses and tensions of family life. We've seen that it can help to take time to sit quietly and become aware of our breathing. Another way of dealing with stress is to become aware of the different sensations in our bodies. Some people find a great way to relax is to go for a walk or do something strenuous. But one of the most helpful ways of all is to change the way we look at a situation. We don't *always* have to think angry thoughts - we *can* think different thoughts, peaceful thoughts, understanding thoughts. And our feelings change... (pause)

Okay, so much for finding ways to relax. Now a brief reflection. I'd like you to think of one or two of the finest people you have ever met- perhaps the one or two people you would most like to be like, people who enjoyed being with you or who helped you to feel good about yourself, either as a child or as a young adult - or recently, perhaps even up to the present... Got them?

What was it about those people that was so encouraging? They may not have said very encouraging things (although maybe they did) but their encouragement and interest in you was much more than words.

So what was it? Their listening? Being at ease with themselves? Being relaxed and accepting of you? The smile in their eyes? Their good humour? Their caring and love for you, their interest in you? Their concern? Their ordinariness - no airs or graces or pretences? What was it..?

Now think of the effect these people had? How did you feel about yourself and about life after meeting them...? Can you begin to see the power of encouragement? That power that you also have... That's what you're invited to discover in the week ahead... (pause)

If you are using the optional religious dimension, you can let the music continue to play for that short period. Whether you are using the religious dimension or not, you might end:

You can open your eyes now and come back to the room gently when you're ready, and become aware of your surroundings again...

Let the music fade out gradually - do not switch it off abruptly.

9. Summing up and feedback (5-10 mins)
In this session we've been looking at Encouragement - looking out for efforts or improvements, especially in a discouraged teenager - and also other things like active listening, being cheerful, spending time connecting with a teenager, being interested in their friends and their world - and introducing them to new responsibilities in a positive way. So I wonder if we could have some feedback now on how you found the session. Feel free to say what you were uncomfortable with and what you found helpful. Whatever occurs to you...

Allow time for people to gather their thoughts - there is often significant learning when people have the freedom to express reservations and to acknowledge what they are gaining.

10. Concluding remarks (1-2 mins)
Ask for a volunteer to bring the snack for the following week and emphasise the value of reading the new chapter before the next meeting.

For next week we're asked to have chapter four read. It's about ways of dealing with conflict and with more serious problems that arise. I've already mentioned that parents tend to get much more out of the course when they do the reading before each session. I would also encourage you to look up your plan at home and work at

encouraging during the week. At the end of every course, there are usually some people who have made enormous improvements as parents. Their secret lies in what they do between sessions. Other parents have regrets at the end of the course and say: "I wish I had taken this course more seriously and worked at the skills." I mention this now because I don't want you to have those regrets. It's just two weeks since we started our course now, so it's not too late to take it seriously, do the reading and work at the skills between sessions.

Finally can we have a volunteer for the milk and biscuits for next week...?

After the meeting

Again the questions for your own evaluation:
Did I talk too much? Did I answer questions or did I turn them back to the group? Are group members beginning to look to themselves for answers or do they see me as the expert? What problems am I experiencing? What can I do about that? Who needs encouragement?

SESSION FOUR

CHECKLIST: Materials
Listen and Check cards (one each - photocopy and cut from appendix 2)
Your Leader's Guide.
Your Handbook
Pencils or pens (preferably pencils)
Video player and cassette - pre-set.
Simple snack: biscuits and tea/coffee.
Music/ reading lamp for reflection

CHECKLIST: To be done
Set videocassette at correct position and volume.
Music and reading lamp plugged in and ready for operation.
Arrange with 2 parents (see sect. 6)
Guide and Handbook open or marked at relevant sections.

1. Introduction/Warm-up (2-3 mins)
Make members of the group welcome, remembering to include anyone who missed last week's meeting. Consider doing a warming-up exercise:

The Back-rub: ask everyone to stand in a circle, then to turn and put their hands on the shoulders of the person to the right of them. Ask them to take twenty seconds to massage that person's shoulders. After twenty seconds, ask them to turn and massage the shoulders of the person on their left - each person is being massaged as they massage. The leader can join in the fun - it may help to relax you too! Freedom to touch can also help to relax the group.

2. How everyone got on since the previous meeting (15-30 mins)
It helps to begin this section with a brief recap of the previous session. When the sharing begins, don't be afraid of silence, because many people need a little time to gather their thoughts together before speaking. Make sure to encourage any efforts or improvements. You might introduce this section by saying something like:

Last week, we were looking at Encouragement and the suggestion was that we would practise looking out for efforts or improvements to encourage, especially with our most discouraged teenager - and that we would also use other methods of encouraging - like active listening, being cheerful, spending time connecting with a teenager, being interested in their friends and their world. There was also a suggestion that we might introduce our children to new responsibilities so I wonder how things have been going for you over the past week?

It may help to start the ball rolling by sharing something that you yourself have done. Remember to be brief - and not to be too perfect.

3. Getting in Touch (5-10 mins)

Lead into the 'Getting in Touch' exercise, something like this:

We'll move on now to this evening's topic which is about dealing with problems, particularly speaking personally and using 'I' messages. We'll begin by becoming more aware of who it is that *owns* a problem. If you look at the 'Getting in touch' section at the end of Chapter Four, I'll read it aloud, and you could talk in twos or threes about why each situation is marked P or T...

After a minute or so, ask:

Do you agree with the way they have been marked P or T in each case?

You might then move through the second part of the exercise, stopping each time to ask who owns the problem and how to use an 'I' message or Active Listening in each case.

4. Introducing the topic (15-20 mins).

The video section for Session Four may now be played. (If you do not have the video, you might summarise the ideas in chapter four in your own words, basing what you say on Table 4, but it is not recommended that you run the course without the video.)

After watching the video, you might ask:

Would anyone like to make a comment about the video, or say how these ideas might apply in your family...?

To build on the impact of what the parents have just seen, the *Listen and Check* cards can now be distributed. (Before the meeting, a few photocopies can be made of appendix 2, preferably on coloured paper or card, and cut into 'cards' for distribution.)

Read aloud what is written on them and ask if there are any questions or comments. Some parents may react to the *Listen and Check* method as artificial - or protest that their teenagers would not be open to trying it. There is no need to argue or defend the method, but you might explain:

This method has been used successfully for managing conflict in many kinds of situations, but it may not suit *you*, and you're not encouraged to try anything at home that might feel awkward or

artificial. We can practice the method in *this* group to improve our listening and speaking skills, and when we're comfortable with it, we can always adapt it and use it in different ways of situations - as a couple, or as parents, or in a situation at work, or in the community.

5. Case Studies

It is suggested that you skip the Case Studies for this session as the skill practice in section 6 is longer than usual and you may find it more helpful.

6. Improving your skills (25-40 mins)

You may already have arranged with two parents to help with this section. People are often quite willing to volunteer but do not find it easy to put themselves forward and often respond better to being asked individually. But do leave people free to say no.

We'll move on to the *Skill Practice* now. I have asked two volunteers to be a parent and a teenager having a typical argument about money or coming home late or not working or something...

(To the volunteers:) **Will you take a minute privately to choose some area to fight about and what differences there might be between you..**

(While they are discussing in a corner:)

I'm going to ask them to argue for a minute so that we get a feel for how *not* to do it, then we'll ask them to try the *Listen and Check* Method, where one person holds the card and has the floor and the other mirrors back what they hear, and I'll be a kind of coach to support them.

(To the volunteers:)

Are you ready to argue the wrong way first - accusing and blaming and so on...? Which of you will be the teenager? Okay, off you go...

Stop them after a minute or two and bring them out of the role-play and back to reality by asking them how they felt. Now ask them to try 'mirroring.'

Okay, we'll imagine it's an hour later, and you had agreed to sit down and talk respectfully and mirror. Are you ready for that...? My job as coach is to make sure you speak personally, not blaming or offloading or using words like 'always' or 'never,' but saying how you feel and what you need. I'll want to make sure you stop after every

few sentences to allow the other person to mirror back what you've been saying. Also to make sure that you stay with trying to understand, not asking questions or trying to solve the problem. So (handing card) who's going to be the speaker first...?

Gently bring them back on track if necessary - but your main task is to encourage any strengths you see. This exercise is usually enjoyable, and everyone tends to learn a lot about speaking more gently and about the *Listen and Check* method. After a while, interrupt the process and ask the volunteers to switch roles so that they both have turns at mirroring.

Ask for brief reactions from the volunteers and from the group. Then:

Now I want to ask *everyone* to do something similar to what you've just seen. I'd like to ask you all to go into threes...

Okay, one will be the coach, one will be a parent and one will be a teenager. Choose a typical area of tension, imaginary or real, but not something too personal or too tense, and practise the first two stages of conflict management - the speaking and mirroring. The coach does as little talking as possible - you're just there to observe and encourage, but also to bring the parent and teenager back on the right lines if they're not following the guidelines on the card. I'll move around among you and you can check out with me if you've any questions.

If there is not an even number, you can form one or two pairs who will not have a coach. The facilitators can move around and offer support where necessary. It may help to play instrumental music in the background so that people are not distracted by overhearing what is being said in other groups. When a group is finished, they can change roles, but there won't be enough time to give everyone a chance to be the coach. Allow the process to continue for about 15 minutes. It may help to let them know when they have a minute to go and to check out if they are ready to finish up. Then:

Any comments on that exercise, or what did you learn...?

Other questions you might ask include:

What was it like to be a coach...?

And what about the experience of listening and checking out...?

People usually enjoy the interaction in the group and find it easier to talk and mirror than they would with their own teenagers, so this *Skill Practice* is usually an important learning experience for all, including for the 'coach' - it is often said that no one learns as much as the one who has to teach something!

7. Planning for next week (7-10 mins.)

That brings us to the planning for next week. would you like to turn now to the planning section just after the 'Getting in touch' exercise at the end of chapter four. You could take a minute or two to read the suggestions there and to plan for next week. One suggestion is that you have some kind of not-too-formal sit-down session to listen and talk through something with a teenager. If you do, see if you can agree on some groundrules first, like 'One person has the floor at a time and the other tries to sum up what they hear.' Your teenager may not be able to do that, but if *you* can do it, you'll be providing a model that will begin to change the atmosphere in your home. So look at the planning section now and you may like to write down what you plan...

After one or two minutes you can continue:

Maybe you'd like to talk in pairs about your plan now and to tell each other what you intend to do.

Couples may prefer to plan together at this stage.

After a further two minutes you could move on to the relaxation time.

8. Relaxation and Reflection (about 5 mins)

Change the lighting and play music softly as usual. Read the following passage slowly, stopping for about 15 seconds at each 'pause.'

We're going to change the atmosphere a little now (dimming lights, and lighting a reading lamp or candle) so you could just make yourselves comfortable and relax. You're asked to sit comfortably, perhaps keep your back straight and put both feet on the ground so that you're more grounded - close your eyes if that helps, and take half a minute now to become aware of your breathing as you breathe more deeply and slowly... Now, take a moment to become aware of a peaceful place where you sometimes like to be, maybe in the mountains or near trees or beside the sea... (pause) Look at the scene, take in the beauty all around you and enjoy the scenery... (pause) Feel the wind or the sun on your face... (pause) What noises can you hear from birds or water or the leaves rustling...? (pause) Breathe more slowly and let the relaxation spread through your body... (pause)

And that's another way that may help some of you to lessen tension when you pull out of an argument or find yourself stressed with what's happening in your family. So far we've tried breathing, then becoming aware of the different sensations in our bodies, last week thinking different thoughts. And one way of thinking different thoughts is what we've just done - thinking of a peaceful scene. Different things help different people, and by experimenting you'll find what helps *you* to deal with stress... (pause.)

If you are using the optional religious dimension, you can let the music continue to play for that short period. Whether you are using the religious dimension or not, you might end:

You can open your eyes now and come back to the room gently when you're ready, and become aware of your surroundings again...

Let the music fade out gradually - do not switch it off abruptly.

9. Summing up and feedback (5-10 mins)
In this session we've been looking at 'I'-messages and problem solving, particularly the Listen and Check method. So I wonder if we can have some feedback now on how you found the session. Feel free to say what you were uncomfortable with and what you found helpful. Whatever occurs to you...

Allow time for people to gather their thoughts - there is often significant learning when people have the freedom to express reservations and acknowledge what they are gaining.

10. Concluding remarks (1-2 mins)
Ask for a volunteer to bring the snack for the following week and emphasise the value of reading the new chapter before the next meeting.

For next week we're asked to have chapter five read. It's about effective methods of Discipline. I would also encourage you to keep practising your skills during the week. And finally can we have a volunteer for the milk and biscuits for next week...?

After the meeting
Again the questions for your own evaluation:

Did I talk too much? Did I answer questions or did I turn them back to the group? Are group members beginning to look to themselves for answers or do they see me as the expert? Which group member needs encouragement to talk more? What problems are there in the group, and how can I best handle them?

SESSION FIVE

CHECKLIST: Materials
Your Leader's Guide.
Your Handbook
Pencils or pens (preferably pencils)
Video player and cassette - pre-set.
Simple snack: biscuits and tea/coffee.
Music/ reading lamp for reflection

CHECKLIST: To be done
Set videocassette at correct position
and volume.
Music and reading lamp plugged in
and ready for operation.
Guide and Handbook open or marked
at relevant sections.

1. Introduction/Warm-up (2-3 mins)

Make members of the group welcome, remembering to include anyone who missed last week's meeting. Consider doing a warming-up exercise:
   Ask everyone with an M in their name to stand up, and then explain:

**Now we're going to warm up today by singing a verse of "My bonnie lies over the ocean", but it's a bit different - every time we come to a word beginning with the letter b, everyone who is standing sits down and everyone sitting stands up - will we try it...?
My Bonnie lies over the ocean...**

2. How everyone got on since the previous meeting (15-30 mins)

It helps to begin this section with a brief recap of the previous session. When the sharing begins, don't be afraid of silence, because many people need a little time to gather their thoughts together before speaking. Encourage any efforts or improvements.

   Last week, we were looking at Problem-solving and the suggestion was that we might practise giving at least one 'I' message every day, and that we might have one good problem-solving session with one of our teens, using the six stages, so I wonder how you got on with that...?

   If people in the group are shy and find it hard to get started, you might start the ball rolling by sharing something that you yourself have done.

3. Getting in Touch (5-10 mins)

Lead into the 'getting in touch' exercise, something like this:

We'll move on now to this evening's topic which is Discipline. If you look at the 'Getting in touch' section at the end of Chapter Five, you can take a minute or two on that exercise, working in twos or threes. In each case you could ask yourself, not what parents *should* do, but what parents *normally* do. And you might also ask yourself if their approach works, if it's effective.

4. Introducing the topic (15-20 mins).

The video section for Session Five may now be played. (If you do not have the video, you might summarise the ideas in chapter five in your own words, basing what you say on Table 5, but it is not recommended that you run the course without the video.)

After watching the video, you might ask:

Would anyone like to make a comment about the video, or say how these ideas might apply in your family...?

If people react, or are critical of the ideas, please respect their right to disagree - what suits one family may be totally unsuitable for another. After a little discussion, you could move on to the case studies - or move directly to the skill practice in section 6.

5. Case Studies (about 10 mins)

The Case Studies, previously presented on audiotapes, apply the new input to typical family situations and are discussed to help deepen people's understanding of the topic. They are probably the least important part of a session and might be omitted now that there is a video to drive home the input more clearly. If you do use them, consider cutting them short, otherwise there may not be enough time for the skill practice, planning and subsequent exercises – which tend to provide more *significant* learning.

6. Improving your skills (10-20 mins)

You could introduce the skill practice something like this:

We're going to practise using consequences now. I need someone to tell me about a discipline problem with one child that they would like to handle more effectively - a situation where you are being ignored or disobeyed or your rights are not being respected...

Right, will you tell us what the problem is...? What do you normally do and say in this situation...? Okay, will you pretend you're your teenager for a minute, and I'll be you - so that we all get a clearer grasp of the situation before we try to solve it...

This role-play can be done by the parent with the problem and another parent in the group if you do not wish to do it yourself. The 'parent' acts in the way just described. It is a helpful exercise in a number of different ways. After a minute, ask the parent with the problem to leave the room for a short time while the rest of the group brainstorm:

Thank you for doing that. Now, I want to ask you to go out of the room for a short while. We're going to try to brainstorm on this problem and see what consequences we can come up.

Encourage the group to think up possible solutions to the problem and write these down as they are suggested. Then tease out the suggestions to help the group decide which solution might work best. Invite the parent back to the room and explain:

I want you to act as your teenager again, and this time I'm going to try applying the group's solution to the problem...

This time, use the method the group has agreed on to apply consequences to the situation. Finally, ask for comments on the exercise from the parent and from the group:

I wonder if you'd like to make any comments on that exercise, or what can we learn from it...?

7. Planning for next week (5-10 mins.)
That brings us to the planning section. Would you like to turn now to the section 'Plans for next week' at the end of Chapter Five. You could take a minute or two to read the suggestions there and to plan for next week. As usual, it may be a good idea to write down what you plan so that you remember it...

After one or two minutes you can continue.

Maybe you'd like to talk in pairs about your plan now and tell each other what you intend to do.

Couples may prefer to plan together at this stage.

After a minute or so you can continue:

I wonder if a few of you would like to tell us what you plan to do...?

After a further two minutes you could move on to the relaxation time.

8. Relaxation and Reflection (about 5 mins)

Change the atmosphere as usual.

We're going to change the atmosphere a little now (dimming lights, lighting a reading lamp or candle, and playing music softly) **so you could just make yourselves comfortable and relax. You're asked to sit comfortably, perhaps keep your back straight, and put both feet on the ground so that you're more grounded - close your eyes if that helps, and take half a minute now to become aware of your breathing as you breathe more deeply and slowly...**

A young tree is tied to a strong stake. That gives it security - something to cling to when the wind threatens to bend it out of shape or to break it. Thanks to the stake, the tree begins to grow. As it grows, it longs for the independence of a big tree and it wants to give itself to the wind and kick against the stake. The poor stake takes quite a battering, but it holds firm.

As the trunk develops, the gardener loosens the tie and gives the tree more room to expand. Then one day, he comes along and takes the stake away altogether. The tree is on its own. But by now it has sent down deep roots and it's straight. It has nothing to fear. It is well able to stand on its own.

Just like the tree, teenagers need security and firm limits in order to grow and develop. We give them great security when we provide a loving home with listening and encouragement. We set firm limits when we explain why we are taking a stand and when we follow through on what we say we will do - in that way we allow our young people to experience the consequences of making their own decisions.

So the word discipline has nothing to do with harshness. It comes from the word 'disciple' - a learner. And young people learn from people who respect them and earn *their* respect... (pause)

If you are using the optional religious dimension, you can let the music continue to play for that short period. Whether you are using the religious dimension or not, you might end:

You can open your eyes now and come back to the room gently when you're ready, and become aware of your surroundings again...

Let the music fade out gradually - do not switch it off abruptly.

9. Summing up and feedback (5-10 mins)

In this session we've been looking at discipline, particularly offering young people the opportunity to choose and to live with the consequences of what they have chosen. So I wonder if we can have some feedback now on how you found the session, what you were uncomfortable with and what you found helpful. Whatever occurs to you...

Allow time for people to gather their thoughts - there is often significant learning when people have the freedom to express reservations and acknowledge what they are gaining.

10. Concluding remarks (1-2 mins)

Ask for a volunteer to bring the snack for the following week and emphasise the value of reading the new chapter before the next meeting.

For next week we're asked to have chapter six read. It's about the Healthy Family. A lot of research has been done recently on what makes a family healthy and what we can do to improve our family life, so I hope you all get a chance to read that chapter in advance. I would also encourage you to keep practising your skills during the week.

And can we have a volunteer for the milk and biscuits for next week...?

After the meeting.

Again the questions for your own evaluation:

Did I talk too much? Did I answer questions or did I turn them back to the group? Are group members beginning to look to themselves for answers or do they see me as the expert? Which group member needs encouragement to talk more? What problems are there in the group, and how can I best handle them?

SESSION SIX

CHECKLIST: Materials
Your own Listen and Check card (for section 6).
Your Leader's Guide.
Your Handbook
Pencils or pens (preferably pencils)
Video player and cassette - pre-set.
Simple snack: biscuits and tea/coffee.
Music and reading lamp for reflection
Ad. for session with teens (see section 9)

CHECKLIST: To be done
Set video cassette at correct position and volume.
Music and reading lamp plugged in and ready for operation.
Guide and Handbook open or marked at relevant sections.
You may like to arrange in advance with two people about the skill practice (see section 6).

1. Introduction/Warm-up (2-3 mins)
Make members of the group welcome, remembering to include anyone who missed last week's meeting. Consider doing a warming-up exercise:
   Divide the group into two or three equal groups, staying out of one of the groups yourself, if necessary. Then proceed:
   We want to see which of the groups is fastest in obeying the following instructions. Ready...? Each group has to have four hands and five legs on the floor..!
   Ready to try another one? This time, each group has to have four hands and four legs on the floor..!

2. How everyone got on since the previous meeting (15-30 mins)
It helps to make a brief recap of the previous session and to encourage any efforts or improvements.
   Last week, we looked at discipline and the suggestion was that we would set limits and follow through on them, particularly for one ongoing discipline problem in our families, so I wonder how you got on with that or how have things been going in general...?

3. Getting in Touch (5-10 mins)

Lead into the 'Getting in Touch' exercise something like this:

We'll move on now to this evening's topic which is about what makes for healthy families, and we'll begin by taking a few minutes to look at the *Getting in touch* section at the end of Chapter Six. Try numbering those eight things in their order of importance to you...

As usual, read the exercise aloud if you suspect that some participants have poor reading skills.

Well, that's just to get us thinking about the topic for this session, so we can move on now to the video...

4. Introducing the topic (15-20 mins).

The video section for Session Six may now be played. (If you do not have the video, you might summarise the ideas in chapter six in your own words, basing what you say on Table 6, but it is not recommended that you run the course without the video.)   After watching the video:

Would any of you like to make a comment about the video, or say how these ideas might apply in your own family...?

If people react, or are critical of the ideas, please respect their right to disagree. After a little discussion, you can move on to the *Case Studies* - or move directly to the *Skill Practice* in section 6.

5. Case Studies

It is suggested that you skip the *Case Studies* for this session as the *Skill Practice* in section 6 is longer than usual and should be more helpful.

6. Improving your skills (25-40 mins)

You might introduce the skill practice something like this:

In this session we've been looking at ways of improving communication in the family and perhaps having some kind of regular sit-down sessions with a teenager to manage tensions and talk out whatever needs to be talked out. Practice is essential, so we'll do a little more *Skill Practice* on the *Listen and Check* method now. I've already asked a few volunteers to act as a parent and a teenager.
(To the volunteers) **I'd like you to argue about anything you like - "I don't want to visit my granddad - or those boring relatives" or "You don't give me enough money for clothes and entertainment." or "I**

don't want to go to church any more." or whatever. Will you take a minute privately to decide who'll be the teenager and what you're going to fight about and what differences there are between you..

(While they are discussing:)

So this is just like the previous practice of the *Listen and Check* Method. We want them to argue for a minute so that we get a feel for how not to do it, then we'll ask them to try the *Listen and Check* Method, mirroring and speaking for themselves, and I'll be a kind of coach for them to support them. Are we ready...?

After arguing the 'wrong' way, they begin to 'mirror.' It helps to give them a *Listen and Check* 'floor' Card. If they do not have their card, they might use a piece of paper with a mouth drawn on it, or a piece of 'floor' (a small bit of carpet, lino, wood or stone) and explain:

My job as coach is to make sure you speak personally and don't use 'you' messages, and that you stop after every few sentences to allow the other person to mirror back what you've been saying. So (handing card) **who's going to speak first...?**

Gently bring them back on track if necessary - but your main task is to encourage any strengths you see. This exercise is usually enjoyable, but people also tend to learn a lot about speaking more gently and about mirroring. After a while, interrupt the process and ask them to switch roles so that they both have turns at mirroring.

As before when we tried this, I want to ask you all to do something similar to what you've just seen, except that, when you've mirrored, see if you can also sum up at the end what you each *need*, if you're aware of that. So will you form groups of three now...

Okay, one will be the coach, one the parent and one the teenager. Choose an area of tension, and practise speaking personally and mirroring. The coach does as little talking as possible - you're just there to observe and encourage, but also to bring the parent and teenager back on the right lines if they're not following the guidelines on the card. I'll move around among you and you can check out with me if you've any questions.

If there is an uneven number, you might form one or two pairs without a coach. As usual, play instrumental music in the background so that people will not be distracted by overhearing what is being said in other groups. Allow the process to continue for about 15 minutes. It may help to let

them know when they have one or two minutes to go, and to check out
with them if they are ready to finish up. Then:

Any comments on that exercise, or what did you learn...?

Other questions you might ask include:

What was it like to be a coach...?

And what about the experience of listening and checking out...?

7. Planning for the future (5-10 mins.)

That brings us to the planning section, *Planning ahead,* **at the end of
chapter six. You could take a minute or two to read the suggestions
there and to plan ahead. As usual, it may be a good idea to write
down what you plan.**

After about two minutes you can continue:

**Maybe you'd like to talk in pairs about your plans now and to tell
each other what you intend to do.**

Couples may prefer to plan together at this stage.

After a few minutes more, you could move on to the relaxation time.

8. Relaxation and Reflection (about 5 mins)

Change the atmosphere as usual.

We're going to change the atmosphere a little now (dimming lights,
and lighting a reading lamp or candle) **so you could just make yourselves
comfortable and relax. You're asked to sit comfortably, perhaps close
your eyes if that helps, and take half a minute now to become aware of
your breathing as you breathe more deeply and slowly...**

**I'm a parent, but I'm also a person and I have my own needs as a
person. I'm just an ordinary person. Sometimes grumpy and moody,
sometimes bright and cheerful, sometimes lazy and sometimes
responsible.**

**I'm not a superparent, but I'm not all bad either. Sometimes I love
my children; and sometimes they drive me crazy. There are times
when I don't seem to be able to stop myself blaming and nagging. I
know it's not effective, but there you are, I'm human.**

**And I'm improving. I have a good deal of experience now as a
parent, and I often have good instincts about what to do. After all, I
know my children better than anyone else knows them. I'll never be a
perfect parent, and my children will never be perfect either - but I feel**

more relaxed when I settle for being less than perfect, when I can laugh at myself and keep my sense of humour.

Being relaxed helps. It's not the end of the world if my children don't do well at school and don't seem to turn out well. I do my bit, but they have their own lives to lead and I'm not totally responsible for them... (pause)

If you are using the optional religious dimension, you can let the music continue to play for that short period. Whether you are using the religious dimension or not, you might end:

You can open your eyes now and come back to the room gently when you're ready, and become aware of your surroundings again...

Let the music fade out gradually - do not switch it off abruptly.

9. Summing up and feedback (5-10 mins)
In this session we've been looking at some of the things that make for a healthy family, and we practised the *Listen and Check* method again because it uses some of the key skills for better communication. So I wonder if we can have some feedback now on how you're feeling about this session and about the whole course in general...

After a few minutes, you might add:

One reservation some of you may have is that the course might be a bit one-sided if young people are not *also* learning these skills and open to using them. There is some truth in this, although one person alone *can* do a great deal - remember that I can only change myself, I cannot change anyone else.

But it *would* be helpful for teenagers to learn some of these skills too. And that is a possibility. Built into this course is an opportunity for *teenagers only* to have one session - which they normally find both enjoyable and a good learning experience. We're prepared to run that special session for *teenagers on their own* next week, even if only a few of them can come along. So what's your reaction - would you like that, would your teenagers be open to it, and would the same day suit..?

You may like to distribute a few copies of the ad. for the evening, photocopied from the box below:

INVITATION TO EVENING FOR TEENAGERS

What's it all about?

For some time your parents or carers have been coming together in an effort to become better parents, especially to become better at listening and consulting with you, more open and understanding. Please do not expect them to change overnight in overcoming the habits of a lifetime! - but they are genuinely interested in finding ways of involving you in making more decisions of your own and taking increased responsibility for your own life.

If you would like to take increasing charge of your life and improve the atmosphere in your own home, you can help that to happen. You are invited to a meeting of teenagers. This will be a chance to meet a small number of others in a relaxed, friendly setting. A chance for you to make sure you can be 'heard' in your own home, that you gain more respect there, and that you can have more control over decisions that affect you at home. It is usually an enjoyable evening and may lead to some fresh thinking and a new start.

7.45 p.m. Coke or cuppa
8.00 - 9.50 p.m. Meeting

Decide from the feedback whether to go ahead with the session for teenagers. (The outline for it follows this chapter.). It would also be helpful to explain to the parents that their teenagers will be encouraged to try a *Listen and Check* session at home after their meeting - on an area in which they do not feel understood.

10. Concluding remarks and arrangements for follow-up (2-3 mins)
This is our last official session, but we will be having one follow-up meeting in a month's time when you'll be able to talk about how things have been over the month (and perhaps you can also report then on the effect of next week's session with teenagers). In the meantime, I hope you'll keep practising your skills and putting your plans into action.

Can we have a volunteer for the milk and biscuits for the follow-up meeting...?

Fix a definite date for the follow-up session, if possible, but experience suggests that attendance will be much better if you drop a reminder note to everyone shortly before that meeting - people today live such hectic lives that when they do not have a regular weekly meeting, it is easy to overlook a date that has been planned a month earlier.

SESSION FOR TEENAGERS

CHECKLIST: Materials
Listen and Check cards (one each).
Your Leader's Guide.
Your Handbook
Pencils or pens (preferably pencils)
Video player and cassette - pre-set.
Simple snack: biscuits and coke?
Newsprint, adhesive and marker (see section 2)
Music and reading lamp for reflection
Copies of sheet photo-copied from Appendix 3 (one each).

CHECKLIST: To be done
Set video cassette at correct position and volume.
Music and reading lamp plugged in and ready for operation.
Guide and Handbook open or marked at relevant sections.
Newsprint attached to wall (or on floor) with marker beside it.
It may help to arrange in advance with two of the teenagers to role-play a parent-teen row.

1. Introduction (3-4 mins)

You might begin with an icebreaker. Have one chair less than the number present. The person without a seat (yourself) explains the 'rules' and says something like, "Everyone who drank coffee today change places." You sit down, and the person left without a seat says, perhaps, "Everyone with a sister change places." Next one left without a seat says, "Everyone who went to bed after eleven last night change places," or "Everyone wearing black shoes..." And so on for about ten turns. They usually enjoy the movement and interaction involved. Then explain:

Thank you for coming to this session, which is about effective ways of dealing with family tensions and taking greater responsibility for your own life at home. Before we begin, it may help to have one or two groundrules or agreements between us. Number one, No pressure. Nobody has to talk or do an exercise in this group if they don't want to - just say 'Pass' if you wish. Number two, No criticism of parents - we asked the same of your parents, that they would not criticise their teenagers. Are you happy to agree on those groundrules, or is there anything else that might help you feel safe in the group..?

2. Getting in touch with the topic (about 15 mins).
Okay, we're ready to get into the topic. Can I ask you what are some unhelpful or unpleasant things that happen when parents and teenagers disagree - not necessarily in your family, but on soaps or in families you know of..? I'll start with two (writing) **Shout louder. And sulk - go silent. What others...?**

Jot down in some form of shorthand, or even a single word, the ideas that surface in answer to this question. If you do not have newsprint, it may be important at least to acknowledge each idea by jotting it down on paper in your lap, so that people have a sense of their contribution being valued. Ideas usually flow freely, but it may help, after gathering ideas, to add in some of the following if they have been overlooked - explode, attack (with words, or physically), bang doors, fly off the handle, trade insults and put downs, look away, storm out, - and sorry for self, use sarcasm, be superior ("You wouldn't understand.") It may also be important to include ways of dealing with tensions by *avoiding* them - agreeing out of fear of tension, sitting on the fence, joking, apologetically taking back what you had just said...

3. Introducing the topic (15-20 mins).
The video section for this session may now be played. Then:
   Would anyone like to make a comment about the video, or say how these ideas might apply in your family...?
   If people react, or are critical of the ideas, please respect their right to disagree. A common reaction is that the *Listen and Check* method is too artificial, so it may help to refer back to the less-than-effective 'normal' ways of dealing with tensions which you have just written on the newsprint. But you do not have to 'sell' this method - it is not suitable for everyone and is introduced primarily as a way of practising the important *skills* of listening and speaking more effectively.

4. Improving your skills 1 (10-15 mins)
You might introduce the skill practice something like this:
The main emphasis in the video this (evening) has been on improving communication and managing conflict in the family, so we'll take some time now to practice that and become more at ease with it. I've already asked two volunteers to act as a parent and a teenager.

(To the volunteers:) **You may argue about anything you like - one of you is the parent and you're not happy about your daughter's/son's friends - or their moods, or their room, or the way they use alcohol, or whatever. Or you're the young person and you hate the way your parent treats you or nags and interferes in your life and doesn't respect you or give you enough freedom or whatever. Will you take a minute privately to decide who'll be the teenager and what you're going to fight about and what differences there are between you..**

(While they are discussing:)

We want them to argue for a minute so that we get a feel for how not to do it, then we'll ask them to try the *Listen and Check* Method we saw on the video, mirroring and speaking for themselves. I'll be a kind of coach for them to support them. Are we ready...?

After arguing the 'wrong' way, they begin to 'mirror.' As coach, you gently bring them back on track if necessary - but your main task is to encourage any strengths you see. After a while, ask them to switch roles so that they both have turns at mirroring. After a few minutes, ask for reactions and gather feedback.

You may like to ask for two more volunteers. Rather than ask for volunteers, it may be better to pick out individuals and ask them if they wouldn't mind having a go at what they have just seen:

I'd like another two people now to have a parent-teen row about some other tension. Would you be prepared to have a go, (Ann)...?

Again, ask them to argue the 'wrong' way before you become the coach and ask them to 'mirror.' After a while, they can also switch roles so that they both have turns at mirroring.

Then gather feedback and reactions.

5. Improving your skills 2: Using the Cards (25-30 mins)
The participants should now be readier for an introduction to the *Listen and Check* cards. *Using* the cards is not very important: what is important is what is written on the card and the concept of one person having the floor while they other concentrates on understanding. Distribute the cards and allow a minute or so for everyone to study them.

It's often helps understanding when we try *explaining* how something works, so you might form pairs now and try explaining to each other how the method works and how the cards come into it..?

Allow a further two minutes, and then ask if there are any questions. This may reveal some misunderstandings and raise questions that need a little clarification.

Now, you've seen a few people having a row as parent and teenager and then trying a different approach, using conflict management. I'd like to give you all an opportunity to try that in groups of three this time. In each group one of you will be a teenager, one will be the parent and the other will be the coach. So will you form into threes...

If possible, ensure that there is at least one boy and one girl in each group. Form one or two twosomes if the numbers do not allow for threes. Then distribute copies of Appendix 3, one per person, and continue:

There are lots of common areas of tension on this sheet, so if you're not sure what to fight about, you can choose one of the topics there! Fight about it for a minute or so, and then try the method - one of you holds the card and has the floor. The coach is just there for encouragement and says as little as possible unless it's necessary to intervene. Will you decide now who'll be the parent and who'll be the teenager and who'll be the coach.... And off you go.

Move around the groups in a supportive role, encouraging them, when they have exhausted one topic, to change roles and try another area of tension. After about twenty minutes, ask for feedback:

Any comments on that exercise, or what did you learn...?

Other questions you might ask include:

What was difficult and what did you find helpful...? Can you see how this could be used or adapted in your own family?

6. Planning (5-7 mins.)

If you look now at the page *Areas of Parent-Teenage Tension*, you could take a few minutes to tick it. That may help you get in touch with some areas of tension in your own family, and should help to make this session more relevant for everyone...

You may like to read aloud the instructions at the top of the sheet so that everyone is clear about how to tick it. Allow time to tick the sheet.

Well, that brings us to planning ahead. The suggestion is that you might choose one of the areas of tension on that page that you've marked with a single X - so not a major area which would be difficult to start with - and ask one of your parents who has attended this

course to try a *Listen and Check* session with you on that topic - time for talking and time for listening and, if necessary, some time to talk about possible ways of meeting both your needs in that area. We'll be meeting your parents again in a few weeks and we'd like to think that you will have had at least one sit-down session with them before then on some area of tension between you. Would you like to take another minute just on your own, to choose a topic that you'd like to talk about and perhaps mark it...?

7. Summing up (5-10 mins.)
We'd like to round off this session by getting some feedback from you. What we were trying to do this (evening) was to look at the ineffective ways in which tensions and problems are handled in families and see how we might manage them better. Talking through a problem area obviously doesn't have to be done as formally as we did it during this session - if you don't find it helpful to hold a card there's no need to hold one, for example, but we wanted to introduce you to a method of dealing with conflict which has a good track record of success and which may be useful in *some* form, and we'd really like to know what you liked and disliked, what you found helpful or unhelpful...

Allow silence for people to get their thoughts together. Then, if necessary, ask:

So who'll go first? We'd appreciate getting an honest reaction from you...

End the session with appreciation of their trust and interest in coming to the meeting and participating so fully.

FOLLOW-UP SESSION FOR PARENTS

CHECKLIST: Materials
Your own Listen and Check card.
Your Leader's Guide.
Your Handbook
Pencils or pens (preferably pencils)
Sheets of paper for skill practice
(section 4) and evaluation (section 7).
Video player and cassette - pre-set.
Simple snack: biscuits and tea/coffee.
Music and reading lamp for
reflection

CHECKLIST: To be done
Set video cassette at correct position
and volume.
Music and reading lamp plugged in
and ready for operation.
Guide and Handbook open or marked
at relevant sections.
(Arrange in advance with two people
about the skill practice, section 4)

1. Introduction/Warm-up (2-3 mins)
Make members of the group welcome, acknowledging that some parents
may see themselves as having slipped backwards a bit and may feel a
little vulnerable. It can be reassuring to know this is not unusual. If some
have tried a Listen and Check session with a teenager, they may also need
reassurance that it takes time and practice to become skilled at it.

2. How everyone got on since the last meeting (15-30 mins)
Allow parents to chat together in twos or threes about how things have
been in their families over the past number of weeks. This helps to break
the ice. Ask them not to concentrate too much on the negatives:

**To begin the session, we might break into groups of three and talk
about how things have been for you over the past few weeks. It's good
to acknowledge any difficulties you've met, but we'd like you to
concentrate on the positives, particularly any little breakthroughs you
may have had. We'll just take five minutes for that...**

After five minutes:

**I'd like to open the discussion out to the wider group now. I wonder
if some of you would tell us what you've been telling the small group
about how things have been in your family over the past few weeks...**

Allow people to talk for a further 15-20 minutes, particularly if the 'sharing' is specific. Remember to encourage and empathise.

3. Introducing the topic (15-20 mins).
There is no need for a specific 'Getting in Touch' exercise, as the previous exercise will have helped people get in touch with the realities. The video for the Follow-up Session may now be played.

There is no new input in this session, but the video may help to remind us of the different emphases of the course and it should help to reinforce the skills we've been learning.

After watching the video:

Would anyone like to make a comment about the video, or say how these ideas might apply in your family...?

If people react, or are critical of the ideas, please respect their right to disagree. Remember that parents do not have to be committed to using the *Listen and Check* method in a formal way - that will not even be possible in some families. It is emphasised on the course partly as a structure which some of them will use at home to guarantee a fair hearing for all - but partly just to practise the important skills of listening, speaking more gently and managing conflict respectfully.

After a little discussion, you can move to the Skill Practice.

4. Improving your skills (25-40 mins)
You might introduce the skill practice something like this:

The main emphasis in the video this (evening) has been on improving communication and managing conflict in the family - and perhaps having some kind of regular sit-down sessions with a teenager to manage tensions and talk out whatever needs to be talked out. We'll take some time now to practice that and become more at ease with it. I've already asked two volunteers to act as a parent and a teenager. (To the volunteers) **I'd like you to argue about anything you like - "I'm the parent and I'm not happy about one of your friends - or your moods, or your room, or the way you use alcohol, or your lack of responsibility," or "I'm the young person and I hate the way you treat me and nag and interfere in my life and don't respect me or give me enough freedom or whatever."   Will you take a minute privately to**

decide who'll be the teenager and what you're going to fight about and what differences there are between you..

(While they are discussing)

So this is just like the previous practices of the *Listen and Check* Method. We want them to argue for a minute so that we get a feel for how not to do it, then we'll ask them to try the *Listen and Check* Method, mirroring and speaking for themselves, and I'll be a kind of coach for them to support them. Are we ready...?

After arguing the 'wrong' way, they begin to 'mirror.' It helps to give them a *Listen and Check* 'floor' Card. If they do not have their card, they might use a piece of paper with a mouth drawn on it, or a piece of 'floor' (a small bit of carpet, lino, wood or stone).

Gently bring them back on track if necessary - but your main task is to encourage any strengths you see. After a while, ask them to switch roles so that they both have turns at 'mirroring.' After a few minutes, gather feedback before continuing:

As before when we tried this, I want to ask you all to do something similar to what you've just seen, except that, when you've mirrored and summed up what you each *need*, see if you can go through the remaining stages of conflict management. The stages are in Table 4 of your books, but you can probably remember them - jotting down on paper as many suggestions as you can think of to meet your needs, then going through the list to see what might suit, agreeing on the details and fixing a time to meet again to see how things are working out. So will you form groups of three now...

Give a blank sheet of paper and pencil to each group for brainstorming.

Okay, one will be the coach, one the parent and one the teenager. Choose an area of tension, and try dealing with it in the wrong way first and then using the different stages, but concentrating on the two most important stages of speaking personally and mirroring. We'll have 30-40 minutes, so feel free to change roles and move on to a different problem if you've time. I'll move around among you and you can check out with me if you've any questions.

Suggest having two coaches (or one coach and one observer) if there are some groups of four, and, as usual, play instrumental music in the background so that people will not be distracted by overhearing what is being said in other groups. It may help to let them know when they have one or two minutes to go, and to check out with them if they are ready to finish up. Then:

Any comments on that exercise, or what did you learn...?
Other questions you might ask include:
What was difficult and what did you find helpful...? Can you see how this could be used or adapted in your own family?

5. Planning for the future (5-l0 mins.)

That brings us to planning ahead. Would you like to talk in pairs now and find some area of tension - not a major one - that you'd be willing to talk through with a teenager in the next week?
Couples may prefer to plan together at this stage.
After 4-5 minutes, ask for feedback:
I'm sure you all realise that talking through a problem area doesn't have to be done as formally as we did it during this session - just listening and checking out with your teenager may be a great start, but I wonder if you would tell us what are some of the areas you're planning to tackle...?

6. Relaxation and Reflection (about 5 mins)

Change the atmosphere by changing the lighting and playing music.
We're going to change the atmosphere a little now so you could just make yourselves comfortable and relax. You're asked to sit comfortably, perhaps close your eyes if that helps, and take half a minute now to become aware of your breathing as you breathe more deeply and slowly... (Music. Then, after 30 seconds:)
There's a story about a man who walked down a street in his own town and fell into a hole that had been dug in the footpath. The next day, he walked down the same street, forgot about the hole, and fell into it again. He was bruised and sore. On the third day, he remembered, stepped off the footpath and walked *around* the hole. Better still, on the fourth day he chose to walk down a different street.
Experience teaches us to avoid pain and bruising. We don't have to hit a big toe against the side of the bed too often before we learn to avoid it. Yet, it's extraordinary how we do not learn from our mistakes in communication. Even though we feel bruised and sore, we keep falling into the same holes and making the same mistakes, we nag

more, we keep on blaming the other person and finding fault, we raise our voices louder. We seem to prefer to live with negativity and even misery rather than risk changing ourselves. But that is what this course calls for. It takes two to fight: it takes only one to improve communication. We don't have to keep falling into that same hole in the street. We can even walk down a different street. That's the challenge... (pause)

If you are using the optional religious dimension, you can let the music continue to play for that short period. Whether you are using the religious dimension or not, you might end:

You can open your eyes now and come back to the room gently when you're ready, and become aware of your surroundings again...

Let the music fade out gradually - do not switch it off abruptly.

7. Summing up (10-15 mins.)

Hand out blank pages and pencils. Better still if you have a computer and have pages run off with 3 questions:

1. Positives. What I liked/ learned/ gained.
2. Negatives. What I disliked or was disappointed with.
3. Improvements. What would have made the course a little better?

To finish our meeting, I'd like to get some written feedback. I would appreciate if you would write down one or two positive things and one or two negative things about your experience of the course. Just a sentence or a few words in each case. You needn't put your name on the paper so that your feedback can be as honest as possible. So first the positives. What have you gained or learned, or what did you like about the course? And then the negatives. What you disliked or were disappointed with. And also what suggestions do you have? What might have made the course a little better?

Allow a few minutes for people to write their impressions.

I wonder if some of you would like to say aloud some of the things you wrote or wanted to write...

End the session with a word of thanks - and perhaps something special to eat in celebration. Collect the pages and note any needs the parents express for ongoing support. You may not be able to meet these needs, but it may help to discuss with other facilitators how your community might *begin* to meet them.

APPENDIX 1:
ADDING A RELIGIOUS DIMENSION

Below are some reflections, written primarily by Flor McCarthy, which are an optional part of each session - for people who want to include a religious dimension. They follow the period of relaxation (section 8), when lights have already been dimmed and music is being played. These are in the Christian tradition. An Islamic dimension, written by Dr Mamoun Mobayed, is also available separately from Family Caring Trust. The reflections may be adapted for groups which do not find some of the ideas appropriate for themselves.

Reflection for Session One

This is not a religious course, but it is also used by a variety of religious groups, so if you'd like, I'll take a few moments at the end of each session to give you an opportunity to reflect and pray in silence for our young people and for each other. Is that okay with everyone...?

So you may like to do that now, to turn for a moment to God in silent prayer to pray for our own young people, and each other's, as they go through this turmoil today... (Pause)

Dear God, thank you for this opportunity to come together with a small group of interested parents. Thank you for your goodness that is in each one of us and in our teenagers. Help us to appreciate it more. Bless each one of us. Help us to trust ourselves, to discover the natural wisdom that you have planted in every parent's heart. And help us during this course to be open to one another and be a support to each other in helping our adolescent children grow in wisdom and grace and truth before you. We ask this through Christ Our Lord. Amen.

You can open your eyes now and come back to the room gently when you're ready, and become aware of your surroundings again...

Let the music fade out gradually - do not switch it off abruptly.

Reflection for Session Two

People seem to have less and less time for one another these days. They are so often busy, so often rushing. And busy people make poor listeners. It's difficult to get close to a parent who is always rushing.

Christ came to the home of Martha and Mary. He was at their disposal. They had a marvellous opportunity to listen to him and become disciples. And what happened? Martha immediately started to get a meal ready for him. Mary, however, sat down at his feet, realising that a woman could become a disciple just as much as a man. Christ affirmed her and said that Mary had chosen well.

Christ has come to your home. As you treat your teenager, you treat him. As you listen to your teen, you listen to Christ - and you have great power to encourage, and to heal, and to love with your listening - with your two ears.

Dear God, thank you for giving us the power to heal and encourage and love the body of your Son just by listening to our children. Please forgive us for the times when we have allowed ourselves to get too rushed and busy to listen, the times when we've been deaf.

Dear God, you made the deaf hear. Touch our ears so that we may be able to listen to our teenagers and to one another. Touch our hearts so that we may be able to understand what we hear. And help us to take time to listen to you who alone have the words of eternal life. We ask this through Christ our Lord. Amen.

I'm going to pass around a lighted candle now and we might pray for each other in silence, that we will become better listeners and grow in love and respect and acceptance of our young people

You may like to mention each person's name as they hold the candle as an encouragement to the rest to pray for that person. (A lighted candle may be passed around in this way at each session from now on, if that seems appropriate - or you may prefer to wait until the final two or three sessions before you do this.)

Reflection for Session Three

Most of the people who met Peter didn't look twice at him. Those who knew him saw a rough fisherman, busy, not much time for sleep. A man who acted without thinking. Headstrong. A man who would tell a lie without blinking just to save face. As I say, you mightn't look twice at him or think much of him.

Yet Jesus met Peter and looked at him and saw what no one else had ever before seen. Jesus saw goodness, love, sincerity, loyalty, even greatness. Those qualities were there all the time, but nobody had ever believed enough in Peter to bring them out. Jesus believed in this rough, headstrong man and gave him the name 'Rock'. And Peter gradually became a rock. Just as the frog becomes a prince, or the weakling becomes strong and loving - because of someone else's encouragement and love...

You are God's way of telling your teenagers how much God loves them, and cares for them, and accepts them, and is interested in them, and delighted with them and smiles on them. You are assured of God's grace and support to be the special person in their lives who loves them, even when they are negative and discouraged and uncooperative - just as God loves you. (pause)

Dear God, thank you for our children and for your plans for them gradually to become loving, responsible, co-operative adults. Thank you for your plan to make us parents into the rain and the sunshine that will allow our children to grow in love. Thank you for all the graces you have given our children through us. Help us, when we feel discouraged and critical, to make the decision to look for the goodness in our children, to understand them and encourage them and bring out the best in them. At this moment, I would like to pray for the grace to find effective ways to encourage a particular child... (I would encourage all of you to pray in silence now for half a minute for your most discouraged child...)

We make this prayer through Jesus Christ Our Lord. Amen.

APPENDIX 1: ADDING A RELIGIOUS DIMENSION

Reflection for Session Four

Can you imagine how Joseph and Mary felt when they couldn't find their twelve-year-old son in a big city? Can you imagine how *you* might feel? It hurts to care about anyone, but it hurts especially to see the children we love begin to go their own way and do things their way. Our peaceful world is turned upside down - as it was for Joseph and Mary. We can feel so torn and anxious that the last thing we want to do is listen and understand. Sometimes we accuse instead of listening, instead of stopping to hear the child's point of view. Yet Mary's first comment was not an accusation but a question: "Son, why have you done this to us?" She asked why. (Brief pause)

At times, too, we can be so anxious about a problem that we deal with it by bossing, scolding, threatening, shouting and so on. We can learn from Mary's gentle approach: "See how worried your father and I have been, looking for you." Maybe this is the first recorded example of an 'I' message, for she said how she was feeling instead of scolding - "See how worried your father and I have been, looking for you." (Pause...)

In spite of the pain it had caused, this incident had the effect of bringing them closer together as a family. They each learned something from it. Jesus came to appreciate how much Mary and Joseph cared about him, so he willingly obeyed them. And Mary and Joseph began to realise what a special child he was, so they gave him scope to grow, even though it meant that he was growing from them. As so often happens, a serious problem had become a great blessing... (Brief pause)

Dear God, thank you for loving and caring about us since before we were born. Thank you for the many ways in which you have respected us, especially in allowing us to find solutions to our own problems. Please forgive us for the times when we tried to solve problems without listening, without speaking our values and without respecting our children. Help us to be open to your Spirit so that we may help our children grow in wisdom, in stature and in favour in Christ Jesus Our Lord. Amen.

Perhaps we might all link hands as we recite the Lord's Prayer in common.

Reflection for Session Five

Our children are our disciples. And it may help to remember that even Jesus wasn't a hundred percent successful with his disciples. They squabbled among themselves, they let him down, they even ran away and denied him. One of them betrayed him. That might encourage us to settle for less than perfection and not to judge our discipline on how our children turn out.

Let's finish by listening to the words of Scripture, from Ephesians:

"Parents, do not treat your children in such a way as to make them angry. Instead, raise them with Christian discipline and instruction" (repeat).

Dear God, Thank you for being our strength and support against the cold winds of life. Thank you for our children and for your plan for them to grow and become strong with our support. Help us to know when to be strong and firm and when to be gentle and yielding so that they will grow strong and sturdy in Jesus Christ. We make this prayer through Christ Our Lord. Amen.

Reflection for Session Six

Sometimes I get confused. I know the old ways of bringing up children don't work so well today. But the new ways don't always work either. It's confusing. There isn't much support around for parents, and I often feel on my own. It makes me angry.

Angry with you too, God. Sometimes I think you're not interested in ordinary, imperfect people who don't match up to your teaching. I forget that you love me no matter how I fail to match up - that you've more time for the poor than for the rich. Well, I'm poor. I feel lost a lot of the time. Will you help me? Will you help me with my children? After all, they're more yours than mine. They came from you, and they'll go back to you. I know I often forget that. I often act as if everything depended on me. So I entrust them now into your hands.

I know you'd love families to be healthy and close. But I'm not sure if my family will ever be like that. All the arguing and bickering and fighting tires me. But I want to stop blaming myself for all that. Just being guilty gets me nowhere. I know you don't judge by results but by the effort I make. I'm doing my best. And I'm going to go on doing my best.

That's about all I want to say. Except thanks. Thanks for my children. Thanks for this course and all the people on it. Thanks for listening. And thanks for your help. Through Jesus Christ Our Lord.

Reflection for Follow-up Session for Parents

There are many examples in scripture of people who balked at change. One of them is the man at the pool by the Sheep Gate in Jerusalem. For thirty-eight years he had been blaming others for not carrying him into the pool in time. Jesus had to ask him "Do you want to be healed?" Do you want to remain in your present situation? He asks us the same question. "Do you *want* to change?" Do you want to improve your communication? Do you want to learn to deal with conflict differently in your family...? Let us turn to him now in silence and open ourselves to the healing he offers - but we have to *want* to change and be *willing* to walk down a different street...

And let us pray for each other and our families - all these people who have journeyed with us for the past few months... (pause) Through Christ Our Lord, Amen.

APPENDIX 2: SAMPLE LETTER FROM A SCHOOL
(Feel free to use or adapt as you wish)

Dear parents,

I am conscious that it can be much more difficult to bring up teenagers today because times have changed so much, so I am pleased to tell you that we are hoping shortly to run a 'Parenting Teenagers' Programme in our school. The programme involves one session each week for six weeks in small groups of not more than twelve parents. The sessions will last just under two hours.

This is a practical programme for ordinary parents from every walk of live - you'll be welcome whether you're single, married, separated or widowed. It does not propose to give easy solutions to problems, but it will look at practical, up-to-date ways of improving communication, discipline, etc. The purpose is to offer you some support and a chance to stand back from it all, not to tell you how to bring up your children - I think you'll find great respect for your own approach. There are also many well-tested ideas in the handbook which is supplied as part of the course. And the only cost will be the £_____ for the handbook.

This is not a dull, classroom-type course. It includes a lively video with practical, everyday situations. I think you will find it relaxing and enjoyable, you'll have some good laughs, and you will probably make new friends. <u>Almost 60,000 parents have experienced the course to date and are enthusiastic about the results.</u> It helps to reduce tension, squabbling and fighting and to create a more relaxed, respectful and friendly atmosphere within the home. Many parents cannot believe the difference it makes to themselves and to their children.

If you are interested, please fill in the attached form. Couples usually find it helpful to attend together, so if you wish to come with a partner or friend, please indicate the extra name on the form. When we have details of numbers and suitable times, we will contact you again. I hope you will be able to attend.

Yours sincerely,

(Principal)

Reply Form - return by (date)
Please reserve a place for me on the 'Parenting Teenagers' Programme.
Mornings/ evenings are suitable (please cross one out if it does <u>not</u> suit).
NAME(S) _____

ADDRESS _____

_____

Appendix 3: Areas of Parent-Teenage Tension

*Mark the topics below, X for irritations you feel, and XX for things that cause you greater tension, disagreement or anger. These topics usually give rise to **events** that lead to misunderstandings, rows, disagreements.. It will often help to talk about the event afterwards, using an understanding framework like the 'Listen and Check' method. What single-X topic would you feel comfortable listening and talking about?*

Appearance What you wear, your hairstyle, jewellery, tattoo, pierced nose..

Celebrations How we celebrate birthdays, Christmas, Hanukkah...

Communication You won't talk (or won't back off). What I'd like. What's missing.

Decisions How they're made. Who makes them? Feelings about this.

Driving Speed. Drink and driving. Back seat driving. Permission to drive when/ where?

Freedom - to come and go and do your own thing (versus responsibilities)

Friends Mine/ yours. How much time spent with them. Irritations/ dislikes.

Going out How often? Where? Coming home time.

Health and lifestyle Food, alcohol, smoking, drug-taking, gambling.

Holidays. Where? Who with? Who plans? What to do on holidays.

Housework Who cooks, clears up, cleans, does laundry, etc.?

Irritating habits How you eat/ scratch /dress/ drink/ talk /smoke/ interrupt.. Hygiene.

Leisure TV/ computer. Pub/ club. My/ your hobbies. Demands on my time.

Mealtimes. What we eat, when, where, how it's presented. Atmosphere at table.

Money How much you get/contribute. How I spend. How you spend. Not saving.

Moods Morning? Weekend? Silence/ grumpiness/ tantrums/ nagging/ rows.

Pets Whose responsibility? Inside/ outside? Hygiene/ shedding/ smell.

Parenting Tensions over rules, discipline, expression of affection.

Relationship Are we too dependent on each other? Too separate? What I'd like.

Relatives Visits - how often?/ for how long? Interfering? Lack of involvement.

Religion What involvement? Differences. Level of practice. Feelings. What life is about.

Respect Different tastes/opinions respected in music, films, magazines, politics, sport.

Roles Attitude to women. Male/female roles inside and outside the home.

Sex Dating. Contraception. Sex on TV/videos/magazines. Talking about sex.

Shopping Who does it? Buying food/ clothes. Irritations.

Sports Tensions. How much time? How much TV sports?

Stress What causes me stress. How you react to my (or your own) stress.

Study/School Homework, not studying, schedule. Different goals

Telephone What tensions? Who uses it, and when? Who pays?

Tensions *How* we fight or handle disagreements. What was our last big argument?

Tidiness Important? In bedroom/ bathroom/ kitchen. Towels, clothes, hairs..

Time Your demands on my time. My demands on your time. Time together

Time-keeping Late for meals. Early/ late to bed and to rise.

Work Not having work. Finding work. Hours of work. Who does housework?

Another area (that irritates or annoys me)....

Appendix 4: The 'Floor' Card

You may photocopy this page, preferably on coloured paper or card, and have 'cards' cut out for session four.

The *Listen and Check* 'Floor' Card (Speaker has 'floor' and holds card)

As a Speaker...
- I make my *own* position clear.
- I avoid 'you' statements, accusing or blaming you.
- I stop often to let you sum up.
- I hand over the card when I've spoken and been heard several times.

As a Listener...
- I mentally switch off my own concerns to listen and understand.
- I don't ask questions, argue, defend, problem-solve - even *agree* with you!
- I sum up what I hear, every few sentences. *You're saying.. You're wondering... You're telling me...*

The *Listen and Check* 'Floor' Card (Speaker has 'floor' and holds card)

As a Speaker...
- I make my *own* position clear.
- I avoid 'you' statements, accusing or blaming you.
- I stop often to let you sum up.
- I hand over the card when I've spoken and been heard several times.

As a Listener...
- I mentally switch off my own concerns to listen and understand.
- I don't ask questions, argue, defend, problem-solve - even *agree* with you!
- I sum up what I hear, every few sentences. *You're saying.. You're wondering... You're telling me...*

The *Listen and Check* 'Floor' Card (Speaker has 'floor' and holds card)

As a Speaker...
- I make my *own* position clear.
- I avoid 'you' statements, accusing or blaming you.
- I stop often to let you sum up.
- I hand over the card when I've spoken and been heard several times.

As a Listener...
- I mentally switch off my own concerns to listen and understand.
- I don't ask questions, argue, defend, problem-solve - even *agree* with you!
- I sum up what I hear, every few sentences. *You're saying.. You're wondering... You're telling me...*

The *Listen and Check* 'Floor' Card (Speaker has 'floor' and holds card)

As a Speaker...
- I make my *own* position clear.
- I avoid 'you' statements, accusing or blaming you.
- I stop often to let you sum up.
- I hand over the card when I've spoken and been heard several times.

As a Listener...
- I mentally switch off my own concerns to listen and understand.
- I don't ask questions, argue, defend, problem-solve - even *agree* with you!
- I sum up what I hear, every few sentences. *You're saying.. You're wondering... You're telling me...*